Initial Communication

> > > > > > > > > > > > > > > > > > > >

When you start to write to someone, one of the first questions you might ask yourself is, "How do I greet this person?" Lesson 1 answers that question. It discusses greetings (Dear Mr. Smith) and closings (Sincerely). In Lessons 2 and 3, you'll study three uses of written communication. These are requests, inquiries, and responses to inquiries. In this unit, and throughout the book, you'll learn useful expressions for all your written communication.

Send Me A Message

Lesson 1. Greetings and Closings in Letters and E-Mail Messages

Exercise 1

Answer these questions about the letter and the e-mail messages on the next page.

❶ Who wrote the letter?

❷ Who received the letter?

❸ What was enclosed with the letter?

❹ Who wrote the first e-mail message[1]?

❺ What was attached to the first e-mail?

❻ Why did Sergio send a letter instead of an e-mail on January 6?

❼ Why did Karen Luce decide to send an e-mail instead of a letter?

❽ What are some of the differences between the e-mail messages and the letter? List them here:

Letter

E-mail

[1] *Mail* is a noncount noun. *Letter* and *package* are countable nouns. "I received a package and two letters in the mail." *E-mail* is both countable and noncount. *Message* is countable. "Do you have e-mail?" "I got six e-mails." "I got six e-mail messages."

Letter

Sergio Carvalho
Figueredo Magalhaes 371/80
Sao Paolo, Brazil 01421

January 6, 200X

Karen Luce
Admissions Director
International Training Program
Box 354232
Seattle, WA 98195

Dear Ms. Luce:

Enclosed, please find my application for the International Training Program. Please let me know if I need to send in any recommendation letters. I was unsure about whether this was necessary for international applicants.

I look forward to hearing from you with information about starting the program. My e-mail address is sc2958@ispbr.

Sincerely,

Sergio Carvalho

Sergio Carvalho

ENC: application
        application fee

E-mail 1

To: Sergio Carvalho <sc2958@ispbr>
From: Karen Luce
Date: January 20, 200X
Parts/Attachments: <guidelines.doc>
Subject: Recommendation Letters

Sergio:

I received your application materials today. We need two letters of recommendation. I've attached the guidelines in case you didn't get them in our application packet. Also, we haven't received your TOEIC score. Have you taken the TOEIC yet? I hope you'll be able to get everything here by our February 15 deadline.

Please let me know if you have any more questions.

Karen Luce

E-mail 2

Mail To: Karen Luce kluce@ITP.org   From: Sergio Carvalho
Subject: Re: Recommendation Letters   Date: January 21

Dear Karen,

Thank you for e-mailing me the information and recommendation guidelines. I took the TOEIC two weeks ago and got a score of 685. You should be receiving the official score soon, but I'll telephone the TOEIC office just to make sure the scores were sent to the correct address. I will send the recommendation letters later this week by express mail.

Best regards,

Sergio

1.1 Greetings in Letters and E-Mail

The level of formality in greetings depends on your relationship with the reader.

Guidelines	Examples
Follow these guidelines for greetings in letters.	**Formal**
1. Use a colon (:) in a business letter after the greeting.	**Dear Mr. Hogan:**
2. Use Mr./Ms./Dr./Professor [last name].	
3. For a woman, Ms. is more appropriate than Miss or Mrs.	**Dear Ms. Grant:**
	More Informal
4. Use the first name if you know the person and use the first name when you talk to him or her.	**Dear Tom:**
5. Use the person's first name followed by a comma (,) in an informal (personal) letter to someone you know.	**Dear Karen,**
Follow these guidelines for greetings in e-mail.	**Formal**
6. You may use a comma (,) at the end. A colon (:) is more formal.	**Dear Ms. Lane:**
7. You do not have to use "Dear."	**Ms. Lane:**
8. Use the first name if the reader signed a previous e-mail with his or her first name or if you know the person, and use the first name when you talk to him or her.	**Dear Karen:** **Karen:** **More Informal** **Karen,** **Hi Karen,**

1.2 Greetings When You Are Not Writing to a Specific Person

It is always best to write to a specific person. However, when you do not know the name of a specific person, you have several possibilities.

Possibilities	Examples
> Use a heading instead of a greeting in a letter.	**REQUEST FOR INFORMATION**
> Use an impersonal greeting in a letter.	**To Whom It May Concern:** **Dear Sir or Madam:**
> Use Dear [*job title/relationship*]: in a letter.	**Dear Sales Manager:** **Dear Customer:**
> In e-mail, you do not have to use a greeting.	
Note: Do not use the company name	**Incorrect: Dear Microsoft:**

Exercise 2

Write C in the blank for each correct greeting.

In an e-mail

1. _____ Dear Carlos:

2. _____ George,

3. _____ Dear Mr. Thompson,

4. _____ Hi Everyone

5. _____ Dear Sir:

6. _____ Dear Mr. smith:

7. _____ Dear Ms Elizabeth:

8. _____ Dear Jill,

9. _____ Dear, Fred

10. _____ Hello Anna:

In a formal letter

11. _____ To who may consider

12. _____ To: Crescent Hotel

13. _____ Dear Ms. Sanchez,

14. _____ Dear Four Seasons Hotel,

15. _____ Dear Sir:

16. _____ Dear Hotel Manager:

17. _____ SUBJECT: Request for Information

18. _____ Dear Mrs. Jill Lee:

19. _____ To Whom It May Concern:

20. _____ INFORMATION REQUEST

Exercise 3

Circle the letter of the best way to start each letter or e-mail.

1. A letter requesting information from a company called Collins

a. Dear Collins Company:

b. **Request for Information**

c. (no greeting)

2. A letter to someone you know very well, Alex Metz

a. Dear Alex:

b. Hi Alex,

c. To Alex:

3. A letter to a new customer, Sam Smith

a. Dear Customer:

b. Dear Sir or Madam:

c. Dear Mr. Smith:

4. An e-mail to the Fetter Pen Company requesting information

a. (no greeting)

b. To Whom It May Concern:

c. Hi,

5. An e-mail to answer an information request from a new customer named Hillary Kennedy

a. Hillary,

b. Dear Ms. Kennedy:

c. Hi Ms. Kennedy,

6. A letter of complaint to a bookstore called Traditions

a. Dear Traditions Bookstore:

b. Dear Traditions Manager:

c. (no greeting)

7. A letter to all your local sales representatives

a. To Whom It May Concern:

b. Dear Sales Representatives:

c. SALES REPRESENTATIVES

8. An e-mail to Ron McDonald, the president of a company where you would like to work

a. Dear Ron,

b. Dear Mr. McDonald:

c. (no greeting)

Frequently Asked Questions About Greetings and Closings

Q: I have an unusual name for a girl. People often write to me as "Mr." How can I solve this problem?

When you type your name after your signature, add "Ms." Both women and men can have unusual names, and both can have this problem. However, women add a title more often than men.

Example: Sincerely,

Gill Martin

Ms. Gill Martin
Customer Service Representative

Q: What if I don't know whether I am writing to a man or a woman?

Good question! This is a very common problem when you write to people from other countries. Unfortunately, there is no definite answer. Some people use both first and last names ("Dear Susan Smith:") in this case. This is not really correct, but it avoids the risk of using Mr. for a Ms. or Ms. for a Mr.

Q: It seems too personal to use the word "Dear" with someone I don't even know. Do I have to use "Dear" in the greeting?

Yes, in letters you have to use "Dear," unless you are writing a form letter with simplified letter format (see appendix, page 88). Don't worry, though. The word "Dear" in a greeting doesn't express feelings. In e-mail, you don't have to use "Dear."

Q: "Very truly yours" sounds very personal. Is it appropriate?

"Very truly yours" is quite formal, but it has no emotional meaning. If you feel uncomfortable, use "Sincerely" instead.

1.3 Closings

The way you end a letter is very different from the way you end an e-mail message.

Guidelines	Examples
In **letters,** you need a closing above your signature and name. **1.** Capitalize the first letter of the closing. **2.** Use a comma (,) after the closing. **3.** "Regards" is not in this list. It is used in e-mail and letters to friends.	**Sincerely,** **Sincerely yours,** **Yours truly,** *(formal)* **Very truly yours,** *(formal)* **Cordially,** *(informal)*
4. Leave four lines for your handwritten signature. **5.** Type [first name last name]. **6.** You may also put your position title below your typed name.	**Sincerely,** *Martha Hamlin* **Martha Hamlin** **Customer Service Manager**
7. Put Mr. or Ms. before your typed name the first time you write. This clearly shows that you are male or female and is very helpful to the reader.	**Yours truly,** *Lee Sanchez* **Ms. Lee Sanchez**
In **e-mail,** it is not necessary to include a closing such as "Sincerely" or "Yours truly," although if you began the message with Dear Mr. Smith:, you may want to close just as formally. **8.** A common informal closing is "Regards" or "Best regards," followed by a comma (,). **9.** You do not need any punctuation at the end of your name.	Thanks for your help. Jim Regards, Jim
10. If there's a possibility that your reader's e-mail system does not put the address in the "From:" line, include your e-mail address at the end of the message.	I look forward to your reply. **Martha** **Martha Hamlin** **mhamlin@aol.net**
11. If you have never written to the person before, or if you want to maintain a formal relationship, use both your first and last name (in that order).	I look forward to hearing from you. **Bill Cleary**

Exercise 4

Correct any mistakes in these greetings and closings. The people's names are Carolina Diaz, Tom Holmes, Brenda Buskala, and Dennis Jones.

Greetings in an e-mail

1. Dear Ms. Carolina:

2. hi, Mrs. Carolina.

3. Dear Carolina ;

4. Carolina,

5. Dear Ms. Diaz,

6. Hello Carolina

Closings in an e-mail

7. Best regards,
   Dennis Jones

8. Sincerely
   Dennis Jones

9. Thanks Brenda

10. Sincerely yours
    (no name)

11. Thanks,
    Dennis

12. Sincerely,
    Brenda

Greetings in a formal letter

1. Dear Mr. Tom:

2. Dear Sir or Madam:

3. Dear Mr. Tom Holmes:

4. Dear Mr. Holmes:

5. To: Tom Holmes

6. Dear Tom,   *(from a friend)*

Closings in a formal letter

7. Sincerely,
   Brenda Buskala
   BRENDA BUSKALA

8. Sincerely
   Tom Holmes
   Tom Holmes

9. Yours truly,
   Tom Holmes
   Tom Holmes

10. Cordially,
    Diaz, Carolina
    Diaz Carolina

11. Yours Truly,
    Tom Holmes
    Tom Holmes

12. Sincerely,
    Carolina Diaz
    Carolina Diaz

Exercise 5

Review the use of greetings and closings in e-mail and letters. Complete this chart:

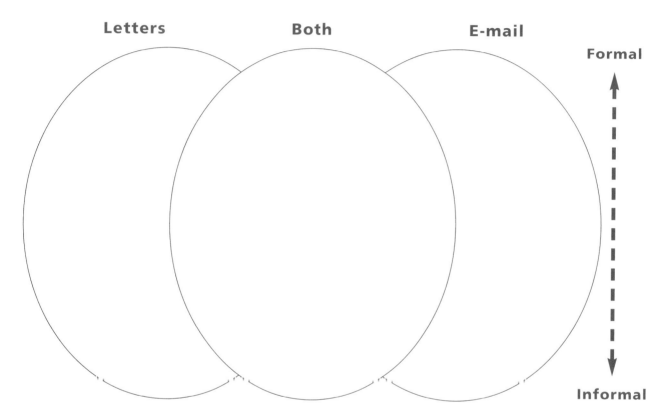

Letters   **Both**   **E-mail**

Formal

Informal

Notes:

Lesson 2. Routine Requests and Inquiries

Exercise 1

Compare these requests. Answer these questions about A, B, and C.

1 What are the differences in the three requests?

2 Which style of writing do you think is the most common in the U.S.?

3 Which style is most common in your country?

A

Dear Sir:

Thank you for your kind consideration of our company. It was with great pleasure that we received your letter informing us about your new products. Our company is one of the oldest in our city, and we are honored to be one of the largest in our area. We would welcome the opportunity to find out more about your company.

May we please receive more specific information about your products and prices. We look forward to establishing a relationship with your company.

Yours truly,

Frances Milland

Frances Milland

B

Dear Ms. Diaz:

Thank you for contacting me about your new products. I am interested in getting more information about the TY298, including the price and warranty.

Also, I would appreciate knowing what quantity discounts you give.

Thank you.

Sincerely,
Martin Bennett
Martin Bennett
Purchasing Agent

C

Dear Gloria:

I'd like to get some more info about your gliders. Where can I see them in the Vancouver area?

Also, how do I enter your contest I saw advertised? I'd like to get that free ride!

Thanks,

Carol Rogers

2.1 Routine Requests

A routine request, such as a request for information, is one of the most common kinds of writing. A request is routine when (1) you are not asking a special favor, and (2) you expect your request to be accepted. In a routine request, it is not necessary to try to persuade your reader because saying "yes" to your request is a routine part of your reader's job.

Guidelines	The Language of Requests
1. State your main idea in the first or second sentence. This saves time for your reader. Include any necessary information your reader will need to fulfill your request.	**Here are some ways that routine requests begin.** **I am writing in response/regard to . . .** **I am writing to request . . .** **I am interested in finding out . . .** **I would appreciate . . .** **I recently read an article (saw an advertisement) regarding . . . and I would like to know (receive) . . .**
2. Use polite, but not flowery language (see the contrast between letters A and B above).	
3. If you are writing to someone in another culture, consider changing your style to be closer to the tone and formality of the writing in that culture.	**Here are some phrases to state a request.** **I would appreciate receiving . . .** **I would appreciate it if you could/would . . .**
4. Be specific. State exactly what you want.	**Could you send/give me more information about . . .?** **Please send me this information as soon as possible.**
5. Close with a friendly tone in your last paragraph.	
Note: *Appreciate* can be followed by a noun, a gerund, or "it if (subject) (verb)." *(See page 18 for more on this.) Could you . . .* is a question.	**Here are some ways to close the request. The last sentence does not have to be long.** **Thank you.** **I look forward to receiving this information.** **I look forward to hearing from you.** **Thank you for sending us this information.**

Exercise 2

Use phrases from the list in the routine requests below. Write the number of the phrase on the line. You may be able to use a phrase more than once.

1. I see from your website that you

2. Please send an application form

3. I am trying to find out

4. I would appreciate

5. Thank you.

6. Could you tell me

7. Could you send me

8. I am writing in response to an advertisement

9. Could you help me with this?

10. Please send us

11. I am interested in

12. I recently received your letter

_____
offer summer travel-study programs. I am interested in your art history tour through France and would like to know if I need to be fluent in French.

_____ receiving this information as well as an application form for the program.

Thank you.

Patricia Denton

_____ for your travel-study program. Is it possible for a family to participate in the program? We have two children, ages 8 and 11.

_____ any relevant information at the address above.

Thank you.

Sincerely yours,
Michael Lee
Michael Lee

_____ who sells your products in the Washington, D.C. area? Also, I'd like to know how much the "Living Water" system costs.

_____

Sam Rivkin

Hello,

_____ where on your website I can get a price quote with a discount from one of the travel clubs I belong to. _____

Thank you,
Yu-lan Yee

_____ finding out more about your university. _____
_____ your catalogue at the address above?

Thank you for sending me this information.

Sincerely,
Antonio Rossi
Antonio Rossi

_____ regarding job opportunities for Japanese speakers. I am interested in applying for one of these positions. _____ to the address above.

_____.

Sincerely yours,
Hideko Sato
Hideko Sato

Exercise 3

Complete a routine request. Each item below represents one part of a routine request. Circle the letter of the sentence that is the best choice for that part.

1. a. Subject: Please send information about your product

b. Request for Information

c. PLEASE SEND ME A PRICE LIST

2. a. Thank you in advance for your kind attention to my inquiry.

b. I am writing to find out more information about your products.

c. Hello, this is Fredericka, and I'd like to find out more about the PDA.

3. a. Send me information about how to place an order for your PDA (model number 4738).

b. I would be very grateful to receive information about how to place an order for your PDA (model number 4730).

c. Please send me information about how to place an order for your PDA (model number 4738).

4. a. Thank you.

b. I deeply appreciate your kind consideration of our request.

c. I would appreciate you send me this information.

Exercise 4

Write a routine inquiry or request for one of the following situations.

1. Land's End, Inc. sells casual clothing by mail. You want to be on their mailing list so that you receive all their catalogues.

2. You read about a new art exhibit on the Boston Museum of Art's website. Send an e-mail to ask about the dates and cost of tickets.

Lesson 3. Non-Routine Requests

Exercise 1

Compare these requests. Answer the questions about A and B.

1 Would you feel differently about the writers of these two requests? If so, why?

2 Underline the language choices that make one letter have a *better tone* than the other.

A

Sergio Carvalho
Figueredo Magalhaes 371/8o
Sao Paolo, Brazil 01421

May 26, 200X

Karen Luce
Admissions Director
International Training Program
Box 354232
Seattle, WA 98195

Dear Ms. Luce:

I was very happy to receive the letter of acceptance from your program a few weeks ago. I have made arrangements for my trip. I will be arriving at the airport on September 5 and am wondering if someone from the program would be able to meet me at the airport. The flight is AA395 and is scheduled to arrive at 2:45 p.m.

I will have my wife and two small children with me, so I appreciate any help you could provide with this.

Sincerely,

Sergio Carvalho

Sergio Carvalho

B

Mail To: Karen Luce kluce@ITP.org	From: Alison Gibson
Subject: Airport Transportation	Date: April 25, 200X

Karen,

Glad to hear I got accepted. Please arrange for someone to pick me up at the airport on the 6th at 4:15 (UA293).

Thanks,

Alison

3.1 Tone and Language Choice in Writing Requests

Guidelines	Examples
Writing Routine Requests When writing routine requests, state the request directly, but politely. Use phrases like these:	**Direct** > Please send me information about . . . > I'd like to receive information about . . . > I am writing to request information about . . . **Less Direct** > Could you tell me how much . . . > I would appreciate receiving a price list.
Writing Non-Routine Requests When writing non-routine requests, state the request indirectly. *Could, would, do you think you could,* and *I would appreciate it if you* are "distancers" or "softeners." They make the request more indirect. The harder the favor is to ask, the more indirect it should be.	**Less Direct** > Would it be possible to . . . > Could you please . . . > Do you think you could (possibly) . . . > Would you mind sending me another . . . > I would appreciate your help with . . . > We were wondering if you would be willing to . . . > I was wondering if you would mind sending . . . > I would appreciate it if you would/could send this as soon as possible. > I'm writing to ask you a favor. Do you think you could . . . > If you could share this information with us, we would really appreciate it.
Closing Sentences in Non-Routine Requests The last sentences in non-routine requests express appreciation or thanks.	> Thank you very much. > Thank you very much for your help. > Thank you for your assistance with this request. > I appreciate your help/assistance with this. > I sincerely/really *(informal)* appreciate your help.

Lesson 3

Exercise 2

Complete these requests. For each request, circle the letter of the best statement of the request and the letter of the best closing.

1. A request to add your name to a mailing list

    a. Please add my name to your company's mailing list.

    b. I would appreciate it if you could add my name to your mailing list.

    c. Thank you.

    d. I sincerely appreciate your adding my name to your mailing list.

2. A request for information

    a. I would like to get program information and an application.

    b. Do you think it would be possible to send me program information and an application?

    c. Thank you.

    d. Thank you for your assistance with this request.

3. A request to begin a program a week late

    a. Would it be possible for me to begin your program on October 7?

    b. I'd like to begin your program on October 7.

    c. Thank you.

    d. Thank you for considering my request.

4. A request for a job interview

    a. I would appreciate it if I could meet with someone for an interview.

    b. I would like to meet with someone for an interview.

    c. Thanks.

    d. Thank you very much.

3.2 Use of Nouns, Gerunds, and If Clauses

Some of the expressions used in requests and thanks are followed by specific word forms.

Guidelines	Examples
Appreciate and *thank you for* are followed by a noun or a gerund (verb + *ing*).	**Thanks** > I appreciate your <u>help</u>. *(noun)* > Thank you for your <u>help</u>. *(noun)* > I appreciate your <u>helping</u> me. *(gerund)* > Thank you for <u>helping</u> me. *(gerund)* **Requests** > I would appreciate your <u>help</u> with this.
Appreciate it in a request is followed by an if clause with *would* or *could*.	> I would appreciate your <u>sending</u> me the information as soon as possible. > We would appreciate **it <u>if you would bill</u>** us in 60 days. *(if clause)* > I would appreciate **it <u>if you could send</u>** this as soon as possible. *(if clause)*
Would you mind is followed by a gerund (verb + *ing*) or by an if clause.	> Would you mind <u>e-mailing</u> me when you ship the order? *(gerund)* > Would you mind <u>if I gave</u> your name to my colleague? *(if clause)*
Would it be possible is followed by an infinitive (*to* + verb).	> Would it be possible <u>to start</u> a week late? *(infinitive)* > Would it be possible <u>for you to send</u> me...? *(infinitive with a subject)*

Exercise 3

Complete these requests. Write the letter of the correct ending in the blank.

1. I would appreciate it if you _____.

2. Would it be possible _____?

3. Would you mind _____?

4. I would appreciate _____.

5. I was wondering _____.

6. Thank you _____.

7. I appreciate _____.

8. If you could help me with this, I _____.

a. if it would be possible to arrive a day late for the program

b. your help

c. would really appreciate it

d. could help me with this

e. sending it by express delivery

f. to have someone meet me

g. it if someone could meet with me

h. for your help

Exercise 4

Rewrite the request or closing line for each situation. The reader's position is listed in parentheses.

1. (a school administrator)
You put me in Level 2 instead of Level 3. Register me for the correct course.

_____

2. (someone who answers the mail in a company)
I need this information as soon as possible.

_____

3. (a program office)
I would greatly appreciate it if you could send me a copy of your program brochure.

_____

4. (your teacher)
I'm having trouble with something in class. Meet with me to explain it.

_____

I greatly appreciate your kindness and support as well as your willingness to meet with me.

_____

5. (the president of your company)
I want to interview you for our company newsletter.

_____

Thanks.

_____

Exercise 5

Write an e-mail message for each of the following requests.

1. You're going on a business trip. Send an e-mail message to the Pan Pacific Hotel in Vancouver, British Columbia. Request a single room for two nights (give specific dates) and ask for information on cost.

2. You're going on your honeymoon. Send an e-mail message to the Pan Pacific Hotel in Vancouver, British Columbia. Request the honeymoon suite, but ask for the same price as a regular double room.

UNIT **2**

Complaints and Responses

> >

This unit presents writing techniques and two additional common uses of written communication. In Lesson 4, you will learn format and mechanics of letters and e-mail. In Lessons 5 and 6, you will study and practice writing complaints and responses to requests, inquiries, and complaints.

Lesson 4. Format and Mechanics of Letters and E-Mail Messages

Exercise 1

Letters B and C are examples of correct letter format. Letter A has several mistakes. Circle the mistakes in letter A.

A

October 4, 200X

Melanie Borg
3 Clover Lane
Paris, KY 40291

Kris Presley, President
Presley Associates
1400 1st Avenue
Mountain View, CA 94043

Dear Ms. Presley:

]0000]]00000000000 0000000000000000. 0000 0
xxxxxx xxx xxx.
  xxxxx xxxx xxxx xxxxxxxxxxxxx.
xxxx xxxxx x xxxxxxxx xxxx xx.xxx xxxx xxxx
xx xxxxxxxx xxxxx .

x xxxxx xxxxxxx xxxxxxxxxxxxxxxx
xxxxxxxxx.

Sincerely,
Melanie Borg
Melanie Borg

B

Kris Presley
Presley Associates
1400 1st Avenue
Mountain View, CA 94043

October 18, 200X

Marcia Harris
280 E. Lansing Street #201
Paris, KY 40291

Dear Ms. Harris:

Thank you for your letter of October 4 regarding the xxxxxx. x xxxxx xxxxxxxxxxx.

xxxxxx. x xxxxx xxxx x xxxxxxx xx xxxx. xxx x xxxxxx. xxxxx. x xxxxx xxxxxxxxxx x xxxxxxx xx xxxxxx. x xxxx

xxxxxx. x xxxxx xxxxxxxxxx x xxxxxxx x.

Yours truly,
Kris Presley
Kris Presley
President

C

280 E. Lansing Street
Paris, KY 40291
October 4, 200X

Kris Presley, President
Presley Associates
1400 1st Avenue
Mountain View, CA 94043

Dear Ms. Presley:

xxxxx xxxxxxxxxx xxxxxxxxxxxx xxxx x
xxxxxx xxx xxxxxxxxxxx xx xxxx .

xxxxx xxxx xxxx xxxxxxxxxxxxxx xxxxxxxxx
xxx xx.xxx xxxx xxxx xx xxxxxxxx xxxxx .

x xxxxx xxxxxxx xxxxxxxxxxxxxxxx x.

Sincerely,
Marcia Harris
Marcia Harris

4.1 Paragraphs

Use paragraphs, not separate sentences, to communicate unless you are making a list.

Guidelines

Paragraph *(correct)*

Please complete the information on the form. In two weeks, you will receive a letter with the details of your trip and a confirmation number. If you need to make any changes, please let us know as soon as possible.

Separate Sentences *(incorrect)*

Please complete the enclosed form.
In two weeks, you will receive a letter with the details of your trip and a confirmation number.
If you need to make any changes, please let us know as soon as possible.

List

Here are the steps in the application process:

- Go to our website.
- Print out the application form.
- Fill out the application form.
- Send in the form and a $35 application fee.

You will receive confirmation in six weeks. If you need to make any changes, please let us know as soon as possible.

4.2 Block-Left Format

The most common format for business letters is called *block left*.

Guidelines	Examples

> Line up everything you type on the left. Also do this when using letterhead stationery (stationery printed with a company's name and address).

> Skip one line between the date, inside address, greeting, paragraphs in the body of the letter, and closing.

> Write the body of the letter in paragraphs, not as separate sentences.

> Leave four lines for your signature.

Company Letterhead
with address / telephone / fax

August 5, 200X

Mr./Ms. Firstname Lastname
Title or Department
Company Name
2000 Street, Suite 100
City, State Zip

Dear Mr./Ms. Lastname:

I am writing to find out information about accommodations and meeting rooms at your hotel. I'm making arrangements for a conference that would involve about 200 people, so I'd appreciate information about group rates, meeting rooms, and catering. Also, please let me know about availability during the month of April. The conference would start on a Tuesday and end on Friday morning.

We would like to offer our conference attendees some options for afternoon and day trips in the area. Does your hotel make these arrangements or is there another company I should contact?

I would appreciate any information you could give me.

Sincerely,
Firstname Lastname
Firstname Lastname
Position

4.3 Modified Block-Left Format

Another format is called *modified block-left*.

Guidelines	Examples

> Line up the return address and/or date, closing, and signature block a little to the right of the center.

> Leave one space between all the central parts of the letter: date, inside address, greeting, body, and closing.

> Write the body of the letter in paragraphs, not as separate sentences.

> Leave four lines for your signature.

Firstname Lastname
Street Address
City, State

August 5, 200X

Mr./Ms. Firstname Lastname
Title or Department
Company Name
2000 Street, Suite 100
City, State Zip

Dear Mr./Ms. Lastname:

I am writing to find out information about accommodations and meeting rooms at your hotel. I'm making arrangements for a conference that would involve about 200 people, so I'd appreciate information about group rates, meeting rooms, and catering. Also, please let me know about availability during the month of April. The conference would start on a Tuesday and end on Friday morning.

We would like to offer our conference attendees some options for afternoon and day trips in the area. Does your hotel make these arrangements or is there another company I should contact?

I would appreciate any information you could give me.

Sincerely,

Firstname Lastname
Firstname Lastname
Position

Exercise 2

Answer these questions about letters A and B.

1. Which letter is from a company?

2. Who is letter A to?

3. Which letter has a letterhead?

4. Circle an inside address.

5. Put a check next to a return address.

6. Where is the date located in each letter?

A

519 S. Figueroa
Los Angeles, CA 90071

October 4, 200X

Mr. Edward Haskell, President
Advanced Communications
3300 Main Street
Houston, TX 77002

Dear Mr. Haskell:

Xxxxxxxxxx.

B

Advanced Communications
3300 Main Street
Houston, Texas 77002

October 18, 200X

Kayla Erickson
519 S. Figueroa
Los Angeles, CA 90071

Dear Ms. Erickson:

Thank you for your October 4 letter regarding the xxxxxx. X xxxxx xxxxxxxxxx x xxxxxxxx xxxxxxxxxxxx xx. Xxxxxx...

Frequently Asked Questions About Format

Q: I don't have letterhead stationery. Where should I put my address when I write a letter?

In block-left format, put the return address on the left. (See letter B in Exercise 1.) In modified block-left format, put it at the top right and line it up with the closing and signature. (See letter C in Exercise 1.) In both cases, the date follows. Leave a space before the "inside address," which is the address of the person to whom you are writing.

Q: Which format of letter is more acceptable to use for everyday business letters, block or modified block?

Either format is acceptable. You can choose the format you want to use.

Q: If the body of my letter is very short, can I double-space to make it look longer?

No. Never double-space in a letter. Leave more white space at the top and bottom of the page, so that your letter is in the center of the page.

Q: Do I need to indent the beginning of each paragraph?

No. If a letter or message is typed, the paragraphs do not have to be indented. In handwritten letters, paragraphs are indented to show where a new paragraph starts. When letters are typed, we skip a space between paragraphs, so it is clear where paragraphs start and stop, and indenting is not necessary.

Q.   How do I know when to start a new paragraph? Can I make each sentence a paragraph?

A paragraph is one or more sentences that all have a common topic. It depends on the purpose of the letter, but typical business letters usually have two to four paragraphs. The final paragraph sometimes has just one sentence that thanks the reader.

Q: I have a really hard time remembering the correct format. Is there any easy way to remember?

With enough practice, you will learn how to format business letters. Keep a copy of the sample letters (pages 86–90) nearby when you write. Also, you may find a template for letters in your computer software. For example, in some Microsoft Word programs, if you click on File, and then New, you will see a tab that says "Letters and Faxes." If you choose a letter and click "enter," you will have the correct format for a letter.

Q: I sometimes get e-mail messages with no capital letters. For example, the message says "how are you doing? i was wondering if you ..." Is this OK?

No. It's not OK, especially when writing for work.

4.4 Addresses in Letters

Guidelines	Examples
1. Put your address (the return address) directly above the date on your letter if you are not using letterhead stationery. You can put your name there also.	See letter B on page 21.
2. Put the address of the person to whom you are writing (the inside address) above the greeting. Leave one blank line after the inside address.	See letters B and C on page 21.
3. The inside address contains the person's name, position title, company name, and address. If you do not know a person's name, put the position title.	
4. You may abbreviate the names of states and provinces in the inside address. Always abbreviate them on envelopes. (See state and province abbreviations in Appendix 3 on page 92.)	
5. Except for state names, do not abbreviate in a formal business letter. Use complete words ("Street" instead of "St." and "October" instead of "Oct.").	2958 1st Avenue *NOT:* 2958 1st Ave.
6. You can place the job title on the same line as the name, following a comma, or on the second line of the address.	**Mr. Paul Brown, Purchasing Manager** **Sierra Design Company** **6942 Marine View Drive, Suite 300** **Palo Alto, CA 94305**
7. Capitalize the names of people, streets, and places. (See Appendix 4 on page 93.)	**Mr. Paul Brown** **Purchasing Manager**
8. Most people use Mr. or Ms. in the name on the inside address, but it's not required.	**Sierra Design Company** **6942 Marine View Drive, Suite 300** **Palo Alto, CA 94305**
9. In the U.S., the month comes before the day. A comma follows the day.	**December 1, 200X** (*not* 1 December 200X)
10. Do not shorten dates in business letters.	**December 1, 200X** (*not* Dec. 1, 200X)

Exercise 3

Circle the mistakes in each letter.

10/9/02

519 Airport Way
Los Angeles, CA 90071

Vision Communications Company
President Marcia Lowe
1400 1st Avenue
Martin, TX 89354

Dear Ms. Lowe:

xxxxxxxxxxx. ......

Advanced Communications
3300 Main Street
Houston, Texas 77002

ROBERT LANSING
280 E. Franklin st.
Lexington, KY 40291

October 18, 200X

Dear Mr. Lansing:
Thank you for your letter of October 4 regarding
the xxxxxx.

Quality Products
132 Madison Avenue
Morristown, NJ 07960

April 4 200X

Mr. Smith
Sales Mgr.
Vision Communications Company
1400 1st Avenue
Martin, TX 89354

Dear Mr. Smith:

Quality Products
132 Madison Avenue
Morristown, NJ 07960

Dear Sir or Madam
New Enterprise Associates
2000 1st Street
New York NY, 10001

Aug. 12, 200X

Dear Sir or Madam:

Dear, Carol

I'm wondering if you could help me.
We have an opening for an administrative
assistant.
It's a full-time position with benefits.
I've attached the job announcement and would
really appreciate it if you could post it.

Thanks Hannah

I can't remember the password i used when i
signed up to use your site. could you help me
with this?
Thank you

4.5 Headings in Letters

Guidelines	Examples
1. A heading is a short phrase (not a complete sentence). It goes after the greeting. **2.** Sometimes the heading shows the reader the subject of the letter. It may also refer to a previous letter or order number. In that case, it usually says "Reference:" or "Invoice Number:."	**Ms. Takako Shibata** **International Sales Manager** **Star Shipping** **1321 1st Avenue** **Seattle, WA 98105** **Dear Ms. Shibata:** **Information Request** **I am interested in receiving more information about the special rates that you advertised in the last edition.**
3. The heading is usually highlighted (italics, bold, or underlined) or identified by a word such as "Reference" or the abbreviation "Ref."	**Ms. Takako Shibata** **International Sales Manager** **Star Shipping** **1321 1st Avenue** **Seattle, WA 98105** **Dear Ms. Shibata:** **Reference: Invoice 2585** **I received an invoice for a shipment sent on April 26, which is incorrect.**

Exercise 4

Write a heading for a letter for each situation.

1. You are writing about a letter that was written on April 16, 20XX.

_____

2. There was a mistake in an invoice numbered 48589.

_____

3. You are writing about your reservation for September 15.

_____

4. You are writing a request for a brochure.

_____

5. You are writing about your account, which is THM2938.

_____

Exercise 5

Answer the questions about the addresses on these envelopes. The addresses are correct. As you look at them, compare them to the format you use in your country.

1. Who is sending envelope A?

2. Do you know who is sending envelope B?

3. Where is the reader's name placed?

4. If there is an apartment or suite number, where is it placed?

A

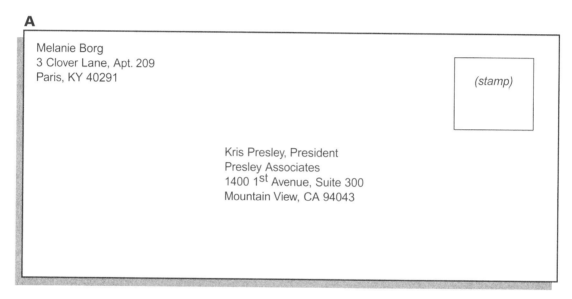

Melanie Borg
3 Clover Lane, Apt. 209
Paris, KY 40291

(stamp)

Kris Presley, President
Presley Associates
1400 1st Avenue, Suite 300
Mountain View, CA 94043

B

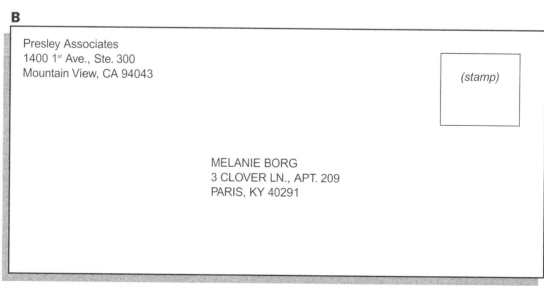

Presley Associates
1400 1st Ave., Ste. 300
Mountain View, CA 94043

(stamp)

MELANIE BORG
3 CLOVER LN., APT. 209
PARIS, KY 40291

4.6 Addresses on Envelopes

Guidelines	Examples
1. You can capitalize all the letters in addresses, but you don't have to.	**(See envelopes A and B on page 30.)**
2. You can include *Mr.* or *Ms.* on envelopes, but you don't have to. You should put *Mr.* or *Ms.* in the inside address in letters.	
3. You may abbreviate the addresses on envelopes.	
4. Leave one or two spaces before the zip code.	
5. Place the address about 4½ inches from the left and on about line 13 from the top. Place the return address in the upper-left corner.	

Exercise 6

Correct the three mistakes on this envelope.

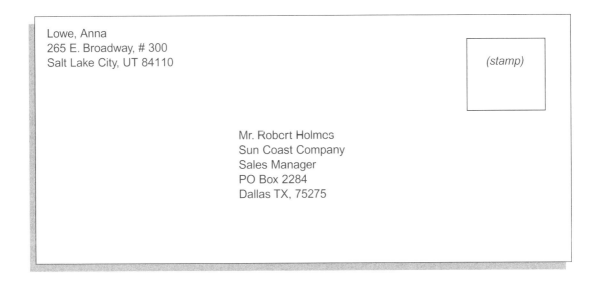

Lowe, Anna
265 E. Broadway, # 300
Salt Lake City, UT 84110

(stamp)

Mr. Robert Holmes
Sun Coast Company
Sales Manager
PO Box 2284
Dallas TX, 75275

Exercise 7

Write the return and inside addresses on each envelope.

1. Write to James Foster, president of the Soda Bottling Association. The company is at 444 N. Broad Street in Philadelphia. The zip code is 19101. Philadelphia is in Pennsylvania (abbreviation PA). Include your return address.

2. Write to Brenda Gibson, admissions director at the Boston School of Hotel Management. The school is on Bay State Road at number 14 in Boston. The zip code is 02124. The abbreviation for Massachusetts is MA. Also, you have a new address. You are living in New York on West 52nd Street. The number of the building is 51. The zip code is 10019. You are in apartment 1404.

Exercise 8

This letter has many mistakes in format. Correct the errors and write the letter again. Change the information and tell your teacher something about yourself.

Stacy Lee

14 Birch Lane
Portland, ME 19107

October 1, 200X

Ms. Daphne Mackey
Instructor
University of Washington
1321 4th Ave
Seattle WA 98201

Dear Ms. Daphne,
I am writing to introduce myself. I will be a student in your business writing course.
I work at the Portland Tourism and Trade Office.
I answer inquiries and manage the information displays.
I like my job, but I can see that it will get boring after a few years, so I am thinking about other possibilities.
I think that I will need to have better writing skills. That is why I decided to take this course.
I hope that I will learn a lot about communicating in writing.
I look forward to meeting you,
Lee, Stacy
STACY LEE

Lesson 5. Complaints

Exercise 1

Complete these questions for A and B.

1. Who are the e-mail and letter below written to?
2. What product do the letters refer to?
3. Underline the specific request in A.
4. Underline the specific request in B.

A

DUPONT OFFICE FURNITURE
463 Avenue B
Tacoma, WA 98064

December 8, 200X

Antonio Duarte
President
Tech Office Furniture
20 Beacon Street
Lexington, MA 02150

Dear Mr. Duarte:

I am writing to request compensation for problems we have been having with your computer desk, Model 182. We started selling this model in May, and since then we have had 32 customer complaints. The complaints have ranged from problems with missing parts to poor workmanship. In one case, the whole desk collapsed when our customer put the computer on its shelf. I think this must be a flaw in the design of the table.

We have sold your office furniture in our store for many years and have never had any problems. The poor workmanship of this model, however, has caused problems both for our customers and for my store's reputation. Therefore, I am requesting compensation of $50,000. Details are included in the attached documents.

I would appreciate a response at your earliest convenience.

Sincerely yours,

Elizabeth Wong
Elizabeth Wong, Owner

B

To: techoffice.com
From: erogers@home.com
Date: Dec. 5, 200X
Subject: Missing Part

I recently purchased a computer desk from your company. When I started to put it together, I realized that it didn't have all the parts. It's missing the plastic holders for DVDs.

Please send this part to me at the address below as soon as possible so that I can finish putting my computer desk together.

Thank you.

Emily Rogers
8503 Greenwood Avenue
Seattle, WA 98034

Lesson 5

5.1 Complaints

Here are some suggestions for writing a complaint.

Guidelines

1. Explain the problem in the first sentences.

2. Remember that you are unhappy with the company, not the reader.

3. Keep the tone professional, not informal. Do not use a lot of emotional words (e.g., *terrible*, *the worst*).

4. You may want to include a positive sentence about the company or your previous experiences with the product.

5. Be specific about what action you are requesting.

6. If this is a very serious complaint, explain what additional action you will take if the company does not take care of the problem.

Exercise 2

The sentences in these complaints are mixed up. Also, the closing sentences should be put in a separate paragraph. Number the sentences in order. Then mark the sentence that starts the closing paragraph.

Dear Customer Service Manager:

(_____) I would appreciate having this taken care of before the holidays when I plan to use the set. (_____) It arrived today, but six of the plates were broken in shipment. (_____) Thank you. (_____) Should I send them back or will you just replace them? (_____) It appears that they were not packed carefully enough. (_____) The order number was SL2837Z. (_____) I ordered a set of dishes from your website.

Ref: Invoice number 349583

(_____) Please let me know how to arrange the return shipment. (_____) Last month I bought a storage system from your company. (_____) Any weight in the drawer seems to pull it off its track. (_____) This obviously is far from satisfactory. (_____) However, whenever I put anything in a drawer, it does not go in and out smoothly. (_____) I would like to return the whole system. (_____) Also, the drawer handle came right off in my hand. (_____) I would appreciate an immediate credit to my account for the return.

5.2 The Language of Complaints

It's not possible to predict specific complaints, but here are some expressions generally used to describe problems with products or services.

Examples

Adjectives

One part was **missing/broken/damaged**.
It is **defective**.
Our order was **incomplete**.
This is **unacceptable/unsatisfactory**.
We are **disappointed** with the quality.
I was **very disappointed** that this happened.
The unit is **too large/small** for our needs.
The quality is **very poor**.
This is **unacceptable/not acceptable**.
The invoice/bill/information is **incorrect/wrong**.

Verbs

We **placed/made/cancelled** the order on May 6.
I **purchased/bought/ordered** a box of staplers.
It **arrived/got here/was delivered** too late to be of any use to us.
Our order **did not arrive** until today.
It was **supposed to** include directions.
It **does not fit/work**.
It **fell apart/broke** after only two uses.
We **have had problems** with the part.
I **am returning** the enclosed sweater because it is the wrong color/size.
We **were billed for** the wrong item.
We **were billed** too much.

Nouns

There is a **problem/an error/a mistake** in/on my **account/bill/invoice**.
The **packing slip** was not in the box.
I think that we deserve **compensation** for the problems we encountered.

5.3 Requesting Action

These expressions are often used to request action in a complaint.

Examples

Please **replace/exchange** it.
Please **arrange for the pick up of** this defective part.
Please give/send me a **credit/refund**.
Would you please **refund my money**.
Please **credit** my account.
I **would appreciate** it **if** you would take care of this problem.

Exercise 3

Complete these complaints. Fill in the blank with the correct expression from the list below.

arrange for	damaged	incomplete	replacement
arrive	defective	ordered	returning
compensation	disappointed with	placed	unsatisfactory
credit	does not work	replace	was supposed to

1. Last month I _____ a portable chair from your catalogue. When I opened the package, I found that it had been _____ in shipping. Please _____ this item and _____ its pickup when the new one is delivered.

2. Enclosed please find a CD player that I am _____ because it is _____. In general, I am _____ the quality of this product, so I do not want a replacement. Please _____ my account for the return.

3. My luggage did not arrive at the airport when I did, so I had to buy clothes for my business meetings. I would appreciate _____ for the expense.

4. Our order was _____. It _____ include twenty packs, but there were only twelve enclosed.

5. The motor on this unit _____. Please send a _____ as soon as possible.

6. We _____ our order in January, but it did not _____ until March in spite of repeated telephone calls to your customer service department. This kind of service is completely _____.

Exercise 4

Complete these requests for action. Write the letter of the correct ending in the blank.

1. Please refund _____

2. I would appreciate _____

3. Please cancel _____

4. Would you please _____

5. We would appreciate it if you _____

a. receiving a replacement.

b. send the new one as soon as possible.

c. my money immediately.

d. my order immediately.

e. would correct this error as soon as possible.

Exercise 5

Explain these problems and request action. Use the notes to write one or two sentences in the blanks.

1. ordered ten portable heaters
   received one

_____

_____

_____

2. sixteen laptop computers
   ordered July 12
   have not arrived

_____

_____

_____

3. a computer online
   credit card
   January 25
   was billed for two computers

_____

_____

_____

4. fax machine
   defective
   model L480

_____

_____

_____

5. ceiling fan
   March 22
   does not work

_____

_____

_____

Exercise 6

Write a complaint. Choose one of the following situations. Write a letter or an e-mail.

1. A company sent you a cookbook that you did not order. You want to return it, but you want the company to pay the postage. The company is Good Eating. It is located on the 21st floor of 2 Penn Plaza in New York, New York. The zip code is 10121.

2. You took Trans World Airlines Flight 62 to New York on May 3. Your suitcase was lost. You filled out a lost luggage form, but the suitcase was never found. The reference number on the form was NL283957. You want the company to pay you $1,000 for the lost suitcase. TWA's address is 900 N. Tucker Boulevard, St. Louis, Missouri. The zip code is 63101.

Lesson 6. Responses to Requests, Inquiries, and Complaints

Exercise 1

Complete these questions for the message and the letter below.

❶ What is the sender's purpose?

❷ Underline the words that refer to a previous letter, message, or phone call.

❸ Does the writer in A apologize or mention the reader's feelings?

A

Send To: Monica Williams	Attachments:
Subject: Tour Availability	Date: Tuesday, May 21, 200X

Thank you for your e-mail requesting information about the August 15 tour of the Canadian Rockies. Unfortunately, that tour is completely booked. We still have space available on the August 29 and September 5 tours.

Please let me know if you would like me to hold a reservation for you on one of these.

I look forward to hearing from you.

Katie Vasquez
ACE Tours

B

Office Solutions
17804 Pacific Highway South
Tukwila, WA 98020

December 20, 200X

Elizabeth Wong
Owner, Dupont Office Furniture
463 Avenue B
Tacoma, WA 08061

Dear Ms. Wong:

REF: December 14, 200X Inquiry

Thank you for your letter requesting information about our Computer Hideaway Desks. I have enclosed the information you requested about quantity discounts as well as the different models available.

These beautifully designed desks are perfect for a home office or family computer use. When the desk is closed, the office disappears! Office clutter and computer equipment are hidden away. And of course, the Computer Hideaway Desk has room for all computer equipment, games, and office supplies.

I will telephone you next week to find out if you have any additional questions. I hope that we will be able to provide your company with our high quality, affordable products.

Sincerely,

Katherine Schmidt
Katherine Schmidt
Sales Manager

Enc: Quantity Discounts
     Brochures

Lesson 6

6.1 Responding to Requests and Complaints

Guidelines	Examples
1. Use a polite, thoughtful, and kind tone. Do not be defensive.	I am sorry to hear that you are not happy with our product. *NOT:* You're probably not following the instructions.
2. Refer to the letter you received in your opening sentence. Use one of these phrases.	**Thank you for** your June 15 order. **Thank you for** your interest in our new electronic dictionary. **We appreciate** your inquiry about our products. **I am writing regarding/in reference to** your e-mail dated June 15. **Thank you for** your inquiry about quantity discounts, which Gail Smith forwarded to me.
3. State your main idea first, in the first or second sentence. This saves time for your reader. Give necessary background information after your main idea.	Thank you for your inquiry. I am sorry to say that we cannot send the part you asked for. We no longer carry that product. You might be able to find it . . .
4. If you include brochures or other information in your letter, mention them and include an enclosure line at the end of the letter. (See the example in Exercise 1.)	**I am enclosing** a brochure. **Enclosed you will find** a brochure and wholesale price list. **ENC:** brochure **Enclosure**

Guidelines (continued)	Examples (continued)
5. You may want to include an apology when you respond to a complaint. Note the kinds of words that follow these expressions of apology: *I am sorry about (noun)* *I am sorry (to + verb)* *I am sorry that (subject . . . verb)* *apologize for (noun)*	**I am sorry to hear** about the problem you have had with . . . **I am sorry that** you have been having trouble with . . . **We apologize for** the difficulties you have been having with . . . On behalf of (company), **I would like to apologize for** the inconvenience you experienced because of the late delivery of our shipment. **Please accept my apologies for** the difficulties you have had with our product.
6. Close with a friendly tone in your last paragraph. This is especially important if you are responding to a complaint.	We hope that the repairs will be satisfactory. Please let me know if you need any additional information/if I can be of any further assistance. Please feel free to call me at 206-543-6242 if you need any more information. We appreciate your patience in this matter. Thank you for your understanding.

Lesson 6

Exercise 2

The sentences in these responses are mixed up. Decide if the writer is responding to a complaint, inquiry, or request. Then number the sentences in order.

A

Pacific Cruises

519 S. Figueroa   Los Angeles, CA 90071

October 18, 200X

Louise Bingham
P.O. Box 571
Harrods Creek, KY 40029

Dear Ms. Bingham:

(_____) If the weather is bad, we consider the safety and comfort of our passengers and cancel the trips ashore. (_____) I am sorry that you were disappointed about not getting to make as many side trips as you had expected. (_____) This is part of the reason that the side trips are an extra cost rather than included in the price of the cruise. (__1__) Anne Murphy at Tradewinds Travel Agency forwarded your letter to me regarding your cruise to Alaska. (_____) We hope that the cruise met your expectations in all other respects, and I am enclosing a coupon good for 20% off any future trip you make with Pacific Cruises.

(_____) As Ms. Murphy probably told you, the trips are only promised when the weather permits.

Sincerely yours,

Nick Chao

Nick Chao
Customer Service Representative

ENC: discount coupon

B

From: Kaitlyn Smith
Date: November 30, 200X
Subject: Dinnerware Pattern

Dear Ms. Marshall:

(_____) You may be able to find it at one of the websites that specializes in discontinued china and silverware. (_____) Unfortunately, we have discontinued that pattern. (_____) Thank you for your inquiry about the Floating Blossom pattern dinnerware. (_____) You can find them by searching for "discontinued."

Best regards,
Kaitlyn Smith

C

(_____) The package contained a return shipping label. (_____) I am sorry to hear that you were dissatisfied with your online purchase. (_____) If you use this label when you send it back, the post office will not charge you any postage.

Ramon Gonzalez
Customer Service Agent

Exercise 3

Use phrases from the list in the responses below. Write the number of the phrase on the line. You can use phrases more than once.

1. Enclosed
2. I am writing in response
3. Please let me know
4. I apologize
5. I am sorry to
6. Thank you

7. I am sorry that
8. Unfortunately
9. Please accept
10. I hope
11. I am enclosing
12. I am writing

_____ in response to your inquiry about air filters. We have a full line of air filters that are appropriate for both personal and industrial use. _____ a catalogue with all of our products.

_____ if you need any additional information.

_____ for your letter requesting information about tours of our facilities. _____ say that we no longer give tours to the public. _____ please find some samples of our products. _____ that your students will enjoy them.

_____ to respond to your April 26 message. _____ you have had trouble connecting with our service. I think that the instructions below should take care of the problem you have been experiencing. _____ if you continue to have any problems.

I just received your letter explaining about the difficulties you have had with the CT203 projector. _____ for the difficulties you have been having. _____, we do not know the cause of those problems, but we will certainly replace the unit. _____ my apologies for the inconvenience this has caused you. One of our customer service agents will be contacting you to arrange for pickup and delivery of the new unit.

6.2 Responding Negatively to a Request or Complaint

The way that you write a negative response is important. It depends on the situation and your relationship with the writer. Your response should be indirect. Be very indirect if the writer is important to you or if the situation is difficult, as with a legal problem. You can be more direct if the writer expects a negative response e.g., in a job search.

Guidelines	Examples
1. Use these phrases for complaints or requests that you cannot fill. It's important to show that you understand the person's problem. 2. State the action you will take or the reason why you cannot accommodate the request.	**I am sorry** to say that we no longer offer tours. **We are sorry** to hear that you are having difficulties with our product. **I understand** the difficulty this has caused your company. **Unfortunately, however,** our building was damaged in the February earthquake, and **we were unable** to start the repairs until last week.
3. If possible, include a positive statement, reasons for the negative response, or an apology.	We usually carry these items. **However,** we sold out over the holidays. **I'm afraid that we will not** have any available until next month. We will send them as soon as they come in. **I apologize for** any inconvenience that you have experienced.
4. Use any of these phrases for general negative responses.	**I am sorry that** we cannot accommodate your request. **Unfortunately, we are not able to** refund your money. **I regret to inform you that we are unable to** give you a full refund.
5. End the letter with a friendly tone, if possible. Note: *I'm afraid that* has a different meaning from *I'm afraid to*. It means "I am sorry to tell you."	You may find that your local dealership will be able to help you with this problem. I hope that we will be able to help you with your next project.

Exercise 4

Complete these negative responses. Write the letter of the correct ending in the blank.

A. A response to a request for a refund

1. Unfortunately, _____.　　a. the difficulties you have been having

2. I understand _____.　　b. to hear that you have been having problems

3. I am sorry _____.　　c. we cannot refund your money

B. A response to a request to replace a product

4. I am afraid _____.　　d. for the problems you have been experiencing

5. I apologize _____.　　e. that your warranty period ended last month

6. I regret _____.　　f. to inform you that we are unable to help you with this problem

Exercise 5

Complete these sentences with words or phrases from this lesson.

1. _____ that we cannot refund your money.

2. _____ for your inquiry about our products.

3. _____ that you are upset about this problem.

4. _____ my apologies for this problem.

5. _____ for the inconvenience this has caused you.

6. _____ the information you requested.

7. _____ regarding your message requesting help with the setup.

8. _____ to inform you that we no longer carry that product.

Lesson 6

Exercise 6

You work for a company that sells computers on the Internet. You often receive e-mail messages from your customers with routine requests and complaints.

Write a response to each message. Make one response negative.

Date: Friday, June 4, 200X
From: Caroline Hunter
Subject: Batteries

We recently ordered 15 notebook computers (Model 2980) for our sales representatives and were planning on purchasing an additional 25 next year. The computers themselves are fine, but the batteries only last about 45 minutes. Are the batteries defective or is this a design problem? Please reply as soon as possible since this is causing our reps a lot of problems.

Thank you,

Caroline Hunter
District Manager

Date: Wednesday, June 3, 200X
From: Kathleen McClure
Subject: Batteries

I just bought a used computer made by your company seven years ago. Unfortunately, the seller no longer had the instruction manual for the computer. Is it possible to buy one from your company? Also, the battery only lasts about 45 minutes. I would like to know if you still have batteries that fit this model (1200) and, if so, how much one would cost.

Thank you.

Kathleen McClure

UNIT 3

Working Things Out

> > > > > > > > > > > > > > > > > > >

Writing effective e-mail messages is a necessary business communication skill. This unit will help you improve your use of e-mail, especially in online discussions. In Lessons 8 and 9, you will practice making suggestions, stating opinions, and expressing disagreement in e-mail.

Lesson 7. Effective E-Mail Messages

Exercise 1

Jim Bennett is the international sales manager of his company. He heads a team with 12 sales representatives from all over the world. Every week, they have a telephone conference. However, in the "telecon" a few team members talk a lot and some never say anything. Jim is sending an e-mail to the team. He wants their ideas about how to solve this problem.

Compare the format, tone, and level of formality of these messages. Decide which is best for Jim to send, and why.

A

Hey Everyone,

Don't forget. I need your ideas as soon as possible. How can we shut those guys up so the rest of us can talk, huh? :-)

Jim

B

Hello Everyone,

As I mentioned in our teleconference on Monday, we're having trouble getting ideas from everyone. Some people are talking a lot and we appreciate that, but others feel they don't have a chance to say anything. I'd like to hear everyone's ideas about this. What can we do to be sure everyone has an opportunity to speak?

Please let me know what you think, so that we can get some good discussion going.

Thanks,

Jim

C

Hello, this is Jim from headquarters. Don't forget to send your ideas to the group ASAP.

Thanks.

D

Dear Team Members:

I'm writing about the problem that has come to my attention about not hearing from all of our team members during our weekly telephone conferences. I invite all our team members to give me their ideas about how to solve this problem.

I look forward to hearing from all team members at their earliest convenience.

Sincerely yours,

Jim

7.1 Tone and Language Choice in Writing E-Mail Messages

Guidelines	Examples
1. E-mail is a quick way to communicate, but do not hurry when you write e-mail. Take time to think about what you say. Be sure that your words and tone will not be misunderstood. **2.** Be specific. Be sure your reader knows what you are talking about. **3.** Do not use emotional language. Avoid negative or angry language. If possible, keep opinions general. Try not to blame one person for a whole problem. **4.** Remember that e-mail is more than just words. It is a way to build a relationship with the reader.	*NOT:* **Jim,** **Just finished our meeting and I'm very angry at how Antonia and Donna take over the whole meeting. I get so mad about the way they talk all the time when we're discussing things. Can't they ever shut up? No one else can get a word in and it's A COMPLETE WASTE OF OUR TIME TO LISTEN TO THEM!** **Julie** **This is much better:** **Jim,** **After our meeting, I realized that we didn't get a chance to hear from everyone about our new customer service plans. Is there any way we could get more input from all our staff members? One or two people seem to take over the discussions. I don't know what the solution is, but I think it's worth talking about.** **Fred**
5. It is always a good idea to end an e-mail on a positive note. People often end with a closing sentence.	**Thank you.** **I look forward to hearing from you.** **I look forward to getting your response.** **See you next week. (informal)**
6. As a general rule, do not use emoticons. Emoticons such as :) illustrate your feelings. They are very informal and are not appropriate in business. Occasionally, however, a "smiley face" may be useful. It can show that your message is good-natured, not unkind.	

Lesson 7

7.2 Additional Guidelines for E-Mail Messages

Guidelines	Examples
1. Choose an e-mail username that sounds professional. Prettygirl@aol.com may be cute, but it won't impress a business person or professor.	thomas@home.com *NOT*: coolguy@. . .
2. E-mail subject headings are important. Use short, specific phrases (usually noun phrases) that quickly tell the subject. This helps the reader, who may be looking at a long list of messages.	**Meeting** *(or)* **Scheduling a meeting** *NOT*: I want to meet. *NOT*: Have a meeting
Capitalize the first word of the subject heading. The rest of the line does not have to be capitalized unless it contains names. Articles and prepositions are not capitalized unless they are the first word of the heading. No period (.) is necessary.	**A Problem with the Cost Estimate** *(or)* **A problem with the cost estimate** *NOT*: A Problem With The Cost Estimate
When you answer an e-mail, the e-mail system automatically puts *RE:* in the heading. This means "about." You do not have to add this yourself.	**Heading of first message:** Information **Automatic heading for the reply:** RE: Information
3. Use highlighting carefully. Some highlighting features do not work well in certain e-mail programs. For example, underlining or italics may appear as $0%.	

4. Keep your message short. Try to keep each message to one topic. If you have a lot of things to include, make a list or use headings within the message to make the information easier to read.	Here are some options:
	    change the meeting
	    have it at a different time
	    arrange for a different room

Exercise 2

Rewrite these subject headings from e-mail messages. Use only short noun or adjective phrases.

1. I have some problems with my e-mail   *Problems with my e-mail*

2. Here is the information you asked for   _____

3. Hi! Tom! This is Anna   _____

4. I want to thank you so much   _____

5. Hi, Bill: _____

6. I'm Diane, who has a problem with the meeting time   _____

7. this is the wrong e-mail address   _____

8. Send Me Information   _____

9. I'm Emily   _____

10. To Jim   _____

Exercise 3

Jennifer Miller is a new sales representative. Her company sells fabrics for office furniture. She wants to show her products to a company called "etc." She sent a message to Jose Rodriguez. She has never met him before.

Circle the mistakes in Jennifer's message. There are at least six.

Date: Mon, 23 Apr 200X 10:55:24 -0700 (PDT)
From: Jennifer Miller <prettygirl@fabrics.com >
To: Jose Rodriguez <jrodriguez@etc.co>
Subject: I Need an Appointment

Hi, Jose:

I have left you some phone messages, but you haven't returned my phone calls.
I want to show you my new product line.
We have some very exciting new colors this season. :-)

Please tell me what time I can come to your office to meet with you.

Jennifer Miller

Lesson 8. Suggestions

Exercise 1

Jim Bennett sent a message to ask his team members for suggestions. He wanted to know how to get more people to speak during their weekly telephone conferences.

Compare these replies from Jim's team. Put an X by any that seem too direct.

1. _____ How about making a rule that everyone has to speak once before anyone can speak a second time?

2. _____ Ask the quiet people their opinions first. Tell the other people to wait.

3. _____ Would it help if you asked specific people for their opinions?

4. _____ We could ask for other people's opinions.

5. _____ Some people talk too much. Let other people have a chance.

6. _____ Some people are rude. You need to tell them to stop talking so much.

7. _____ I wonder if we could establish some rules for the discussion.

8. _____ You have to ask people who haven't spoken for their opinions.

9. _____ Maybe we could have a time limit for any one speaker.

10. _____ People shouldn't interrupt. They are so impolite to do that.

8.1 Tone and Language Choice for Making Suggestions

Guidelines	Examples
1. If necessary, begin with why you're writing.	**I'm trying to set up a time when we could all meet to talk about . . .**
2. Be direct if the suggestion is routine.	**Let's talk about this at our meeting on Friday.**
3. Be less direct if the suggestion is not routine.	**It might be a good idea to talk about this with Jim.**
Note: The simple form of the verb follows "Let's" and modal auxiliary verbs, such as *would*, *could*, *can*. Use a noun or gerund after "How about."	**Direct Suggestions** **Let's talk about this.** **How about Friday?** **How about meeting tomorrow?** **Would Tuesday work?/be okay?** **Why don't we . . . ?** **Less Direct Suggestions** **If you can/could . . . , we can/could/will . . .** **I'm wondering if we could . . . ?** **Do you think we should/could . . . ?** **Maybe we should/could . . .** **I was wondering about whether we might be able to . . . ?** **What do you think?** **I'd like to get your ideas/suggestions on this idea.**

Exercise 2

Complete these suggestions. Write the letter of the correct ending in the blank.

A. A suggestion to meet

1. Would _____?

2. If we could talk about it on Thursday, _____.

3. Let's _____.

4. How about _____?

a. that would probably help

b. work on this and see what we can come up with

c. asking people what they think

d. a meeting on Monday work for you

B. A suggestion to wait

5. I wonder if we _____?

6. How about _____?

7. Have you _____?

8. Why don't we _____?

e. 9:30

f. already decided

g. could wait until next month to decide

h. ask the director what she thinks

C. A suggestion to wait

9. I'd like to suggest _____.

10. Maybe we _____.

11. I'm wondering if we could _____.

12. I'd like _____.

i. give them longer to reply

j. another possibility

k. need to get more ideas

l. to find out what everyone thinks before we make a decision

Exercise 3

Make suggestions about your class, program, or city.

1. Why don't we _____

2. Do you think _____

3. How about _____

4. If _____

5. I'm wondering _____

8.2 Tips for Responding to Suggestions

Guidelines	Examples
1. You can be direct if the suggestion is routine.	**Changing the time to 9:00 is fine with me.** **I agree that we should do this.**
2. You can also be direct if the suggestion is not routine, but you agree with it.	**Adding a price list is a good idea. Thanks for the suggestion.**
3. If the suggestion is not routine and you disagree with it, say something positive first. Then explain why you disagree. The level of indirectness will depend on your relationship with the writer. When in doubt, be more indirect.	**We received your suggestion for changes in the report, but there's some information that you may not have seen.** **Thanks for suggesting that we include a price list on the website. Unfortunately, prices change so often that this is not possible.**
4. Remember that it is never good to use emotional or judgmental language.	**Thank you for your suggestion.** ***NOT*: That suggestion is really stupid. I can't believe you would even suggest it!**

8.3 The Language of Responses to Suggestions

Agree with suggestions	Disagree with suggestions
Direct ____ is fine. OK. Let's . . . I agree that . . .	**Direct** Thanks for your suggestion. Unfortunately, I can't . . . I'm afraid . . . is not possible at this time.
Less Direct I like your suggestion to . . . . . . is a good idea. . . . sounds like a good idea.	**Less Direct** I'm not sure . . . Your suggestion/Your plan won't work. I received your suggestion about . . ., but . . . I wonder if we could . . ./Could we . . .? ____ would be better.

8.4 Referring to Suggestions

Guidelines	Examples
> Here are some ways to refer to suggestions.	Anna suggested we start a new . . . As you suggested, I am calling a meeting to discuss . . . Following your suggestion, I added . . .

Exercise 4

Circle the letter of the best response.

1. I agree ____.
   a. the decision
   b. with you

2. I agree ____.
   a. the move that we are making
   b. that this move will be difficult

3. I'm afraid ____.
   a. your idea is too expensive
   b. too expensive what you suggest

4. A different advertisement ____.
   a. be better
   b. would be better

5. I like your suggestion ____.
   a. adding the address
   b. about adding the address

6. I wonder ____.
   a. you could speak to them directly
   b. if you could speak to them directly

7. Could we ____?
   a. make the change later
   b. making the change later

8. I'm not sure ____.
   a. this idea working
   b. that this idea will work

Exercise 5

Exchange books with a classmate. Respond either positively or negatively to the suggestions he or she made in Exercise 3.

1. _____

2. _____

3. _____

4. _____

5. _____

Lesson 8

Exercise 6

You are Jim Bennett, the head of the international sales team. Your team's weekly phone conference did not succeed. You then decided that the team will meet at headquarters four times a year. However, some team members did not like your decision.

1. Write a negative, but professional, response to this message.

> Why did you decide to bring us all to headquarters four times a year? It doesn't make any sense! How are we supposed to take care of our customers when we're running back and forth to headquarters all the time? Why don't you just ask the talkative people to be quiet?
>
> Dave

2. Write a positive response to this one.

> I just read your e-mail about having us all come to headquarters four times a year for face-to-face meetings. I understand that it's difficult to make decisions when we're all so far apart and have such different communication styles, but I wonder whether we really need so many face-to-face meetings. Is there any chance you could reconsider or have meetings once a year instead of four times?
>
> Thanks,
>
> Martin

Lesson 9. Opinions and Disagreements

Exercise 1

Christina Lowe is a manager in a large company. Her company decided that employees must stop smoking in the building. Christina e-mailed her group to explain the new rule. Now, many of them are e-mailing Christina to tell her their opinions about this rule.

Read Christina's e-mail. Then read the responses. Put an X by any that seem inappropriate.

Date: Mon, 23 Apr 200X 10:55:24 -0700 (PDT)
From: Christina Lowe <christina.lowe@nwu.co>
To: Group <group@nwu.co>
Subject: New Policy about Smoking

After a lot of discussion, senior management has decided that we should have a totally smoke-free building. This means that there will no longer be a smoking section in the cafeteria or smoking rooms on each floor. Smokers are asked not to smoke near any entrances or vents leading into the building.

Christina

1. _____ I can't believe this company has all these ridiculous rules. Are we supposed to go outside in the middle of winter to have a cigarette?

2. _____ I understand the company is concerned about everyone's health, but this seems a bit extreme. Could one room be left for smokers to go to?

3. _____ I wouldn't count on it. Not with all the !*##(s in management in this building.

4. _____ Christina, what do you think? Is there any chance we'll be able to get them to change their decision?

5. _____ THIS IS ABSURD! We can't go all the way down the elevators, outside (in the rain or snow!), and then come back within one break.

6. _____ I'm sorry for everyone who is going to have to go outside, but it will really help those of us who don't smoke.

7. _____ I agree with everyone that this change doesn't seem fair, but I think it's the company's right to be able to make these policies.

8. _____ Come on, you guys, lighten up! You might live longer.

Lesson 9

9.1 Giving Opinions

Guidelines	Examples
1. As with other business communication, negative opinions or non-routine reactions need to be expressed more carefully than positive opinions or routine reactions.	**Positive Reactions** That sounds fine. **I'm pleased to hear that** you have decided to change the policy. **I think that** making this change **is a good idea.** Wow! That's great! *(very informal)*
2. Don't use emotional language or judgmental words in negative opinions or non-routine reactions.	**Negative Reactions** **In my opinion,** it's not a good idea to do this. **My opinion/My point of view is that** it's not a good idea.
3. CAPITAL LETTERS in e-mail are a way of expressing strong emotion. It's a good idea not to use them in business communication.	**I don't think that** this is a good idea. **It seems to me that** this is not a good idea. **I wonder if** this is a good idea.

Exercise 2

Complete these reactions to situations. Finish each sentence with your opinion.

1. I'm writing to inform you that you will have an extra hour of class today.

Opinion: I think _____.

2. To increase productivity, we have decided to cut everyone's lunch hour by ten minutes.

Opinion: My opinion is _____.

3. Because of your team's excellent work, we have decided to give everyone a raise.

Opinion: I'm pleased _____.

4. Guess what? I just saw your name on a list of people getting promoted!

Opinion: (informal) _____.

5. In order to cut costs, we have decided to cut all salaries by 10%.

Opinion: In my opinion, _____.

> > > > > > > > > > > > > > >

9.2 **Hedging**

Sometimes, it is better not to state an opinion at all. "Hedging" is a way of not stating an opinion until (1) you find out other people's opinions, or (2) you have asked all the relevant questions to determine your own opinion.

Examples

Asking Opinions
What's your opinion?
What do you think about this?
Do you think this is a good idea or not?
I was wondering what your opinion is about the new policy.
(Name), would you like to give your opinion about this?

Asking Other Relevant Questions or Clarifying
Is there some information we're missing?
Are there any other options?
Do you know whether this is a final decision?
I wonder if there's room for any discussion on this.
Is there a chance we can discuss this?

Exercise 3

Decide if each sentence is hedging (H) or stating an opinion (O). Write H or O in the blank.

1. _____ Christina, do you think this is a good idea?

2. _____ I wonder whether this is the final decision.

3. _____ I'm glad that management has finally done something about this problem.

4. _____ Is there any chance we'll be able to get them to build a smoking shelter outside?

5. _____ Christina, will we have any opportunities to give our ideas on this?

6. _____ I wish they had asked us our opinion.

7. _____ It seems to me that this is going to be good for everyone in the long run.

8. _____ Are there any other options? A smoking room, for example?

9.3 Disagreeing

Guidelines	Examples
1. If possible, find something to agree about first.	You have a good point about . . . . However, I think . . . I agree with you that . . ., but . . .
2. If appropriate, express understanding of an opposing viewpoint or the feelings of another person.	I can understand how strongly you feel about this, but I'm afraid that . . . I'm sorry that we had to make this decision, but . . . I understand your point of view, but I have to disagree. I . . .
3. State your disagreement with some "distancers" or "softeners."	I'm afraid I don't think that . . . I don't really agree that . . . Unfortunately, this won't work at all.

Exercise 4

Pedro Meghaeles is the head of a management team at his corporation. His corporation wants some team members to go to New York for more leadership training. Pedro e-mailed these people to tell them. They e-mailed him back to discuss the decision.

> Read Pedro Meghaeles's message. Then read the comments. Decide which of the categories below each comment fits into. Write the letter in the blank.

To: Management Team
Subject: Executive Training

Date: March 3, 200X

We have decided that our management team would benefit from additional leadership training. After talking with several well-known training organizations, we have signed an agreement with Executive Trainers in New York. The training will consist of a six-month intensive course in New York. Everyone receiving this message will go through the training, in groups of three.

I'll be sending more information about this next week. The first group will start the training in September.

Pedro Meghaeles

A   expressing an opinion
B   showing understanding of another person's point of view
C   hedging

1. (a. _____) This may be fine for people without children,
   (b. _____) but it's going to be very difficult to leave my family for six months.

2. (a. _____) I understand that it'll be difficult to arrange to be away,
   (b. _____) but once we're there, I'm sure we'll find it a valuable experience, and quite exciting to live in New York.

3. (a. _____) In my opinion, it would make more sense to have the training program here.
   (b. _____) It would cost less because we wouldn't have the transportation and housing costs.

4. (a. _____) Wouldn't they charge us more to offer the program here?
   (b. _____) It might be more expensive.

5. (a. _____) I think you're probably right that they would charge more,
   (b. _____) but it still wouldn't cost as much as sending 14 of us to New York for six months.

6. (a. ___) You're probably right about that.

   (b. ___) We haven't heard from Allen on this. Allen, what do you think?

7. (a. ___) It seems like we need some more information before we talk to Pedro.

Exercise 5

Choose one topic below, and have an e-mail discussion with a group. You can write your messages on paper, using the language of this unit. The discussion must include a suggestion, an opinion, and responses to the opinion. Group members should agree, disagree, and hedge.

1. A new client, Shen Hsu, is coming to your city for two days. His wife will be traveling with him. Plan his visit.

2. Your company is going to move their office to another city. Decide the best place to move.

UNIT 4

Job-Search Writing

> >

This unit will help if you are looking for a job. It includes examples of resumes and letters for a job search. In Lesson 10, you will learn to develop a resume. In Lesson 11, you will practice writing resume cover letters. The final lesson, Lesson 12, offers practice in writing follow-up letters after interviews.

Lesson 10. Resumes

Exercise 1

Find this information in the following resumes.

> a statement about the kind of job the person is looking for

> a description of each person's work experience

> a description of each person's education

Tomoko Martin
8105 50th St. N.W., Davis CA 96515
415-945-0200
tmartin@sfol.net

Objective: To use my knowledge of languages, computer skills, and experience working with international visitors in a tourist-related industry

Summary:
- Native speaker of Japanese
- Advanced proficiency in Spanish and English
- Three years experience with customer service and office management
- Experience with all Microsoft Office applications

Experience: **Office Assistant,** University of California English Language Programs, 2003–present
- Manage reception and telephones for 40-person office
- Develop data base to track inquiries about application status
- Train temporary workers in office procedures

Volunteer, International Student Office, University of California, 2000–2003
- Arranged special events for international students
- Assisted program directors in orientation and cultural exchange programs
- Reorganized office to be more efficient

Volunteer, Shoreline Boys and Girls Club, 1997–1998
- Led afternoon activities for groups of children
- Managed activity budget for programs
- Recognized as Volunteer of the Year, 1998

Education: **B.A. in Business Administration,** University of California Davis, Davis, CA, 2003

Activities: Volunteer translator, Shoreline Japanese Community Center, 1996–1998
Assistant Leader for Girl Scouts, 1997–1998

References: Available Upon Request

Hugh Clark

Current Address:		**Permanent**
3609 Walnut Street #462		**Address:**
Philadelphia, PA 19104		4789 Easton
215-898-5264		Street
		Atlanta, GA
		404-555-5758

Objective: A summer job in banking or finance

Education: **B.A.,** anticipated in June, 2004, The Wharton School, University of Pennsylvania
Major: Finance   GPA in major: 3.5/4.0
Minor: Spanish   GPA (all courses): 3.0/4.0

Relevant Experience and Qualifications: Intern, First Mutual Bank, Atlanta, GA, summers of 2002 and 2003
• Worked in various areas of bank
• Assisted with new intern orientation (summer, 2003)
• Offered permanent position

International Exchange Participant, 2002–2003
• Awarded Rotary Club scholarship
• Lived in Barcelona, Spain, for 8 months
• Studied at the University of Barcelona
• Visited France, Italy, and Germany

Coursework, The Wharton School, University of Pennsylvania, 2001–present
• Finance
• International Finance
• Investments (2 courses)
• International Trade
• Legal Issues in Business
• Macroeconomics
• Microeconomics

Volunteer, World Trade Center Conference, Atlanta, GA, fall, 1999
• Assisted with conference program
• Set up receptions
• Sent out conference proceedings to participants

Skills
• Fluent in Spanish
• Excellent interpersonal communication skills

Other Experience: **Sailing Instructor,** Savannah Yacht Club, summer, 2001
• Taught racing skills to a variety of levels
• Competed in Junior Olympics

10.1 Writing Resumes

Your resume is a tool. Along with the cover letter, it helps you get a job interview. A resume shows what you've done to prepare you for the job. It must be clear and easy to understand. The reader in the company is going to look at it very quickly, probably in less than a minute.

Guidelines

1. Length

A one-page resume is best, unless you are applying for top-management positions.

2. Organization and Format

Most resumes are in reverse chronological order. List your education and experience by year, and put the most recent first. (See examples in Exercise 1.) If you are changing careers, you may add a section listing job-related or basic skills.

Make your resume look business-like and professional. Do not use too many fancy styles or fonts. However, you may do this if you are applying for an artistic or creative position. If not, keep the resume simple and easy to read.

3. Content

Resumes usually include the following items.

> Contact information	**Name, address, telephone number, e-mail address**
> Career or job objective	**This is a statement of your goal. State your goal specifically. Use a phrase or complete sentence such as "A summer job in an international trading company" or "An opportunity to use my knowledge of Japanese language and culture in a small company doing business in Asia."**
> Employment	**Most companies expect resumes to be chronological, with the most recent experience first. Explain your responsibilities or accomplishments in each position. Also include your job title. If you are applying for a job in another country, briefly describe your current or last company ("Customer Service Manager at REI, a company specializing in high-tech recreational gear").**

> Education/training	You may need to explain. Your education and training may relate to the skills or experience needed for the job, but someone else may not understand how they are related. In this case, use *equivalent to*. List your experience or training, then *equivalent to*, and after that the name of the required skill or experience.
> Special skills or knowledge	Be sure to include the languages you know and how well you speak them ("French, native speaker" or "English, advanced level in reading, speaking and listening; intermediate level in writing"). This section can go at the beginning or at the end of your resume.

Job applications in some countries should not include photos or references to race, religion, marital status, or age. Find out before you write your resume.

Exercise 2

Job objectives can be very important. The exercises below will help you write your own job objective.

Part A

A job objective is optional. Put an X beside each situation in which you should include one.

1. ____ You are only planning to work for the summer.

2. ____ This is your first job search and you don't care what job you get.

3. ____ You are applying to a very large corporation that has many different types of jobs open at all levels and areas of the company.

4. ____ You are applying to a company where everyone always starts in an entry-level position.

Part B

A well-written job objective is specific. Put an X beside the more specific objective in each pair below.

1. a. ____ A job in accounting
   b. ____ To use my accounting skills and clerical experience in a job related to international trade

2. a. ____ To work as an English teacher in an international school
   ____ To be a team player in a creative environment

Part C

A specific job objective may contain all of the following items. Write the appropriate letters under items you see in the sentences below.

A   level or type of job
B   specific position
C   skills
D   type of company or industry

1. A <u>part-time</u> <u>clerical position</u> in a <u>small company</u>
     A   *A*   *D*

2. An <u>administrative position</u> in a <u>medical technology</u> firm where I can

demonstrate my <u>strong organizational and communication skills</u>

3. A <u>full-time position</u> in a <u>computer game company</u> where I can

<u>use my creativity</u> and <u>be part of a dynamic team</u>

4. To use my <u>quantitative and analytical skills</u> as an <u>accountant</u> at a

<u>university</u>

5. An <u>entry-level position</u> as a <u>sales account representative</u>

Part D

Answer these questions to develop your own job objective.

1. Which level position are you looking for?

___ entry level   ___ part-time   ___ administrative   ___ executive

___ volunteer   ___ full-time   ___ managerial

2. What are your skills? _____

3. What position do you want to have? _____

4. What industry or area do you want a job in? _____

5. Write a job objective. Start with a noun ("An entry level job in . . .") or an infinitive ("To work in . . ."). Remember that you don't have to use all the items in 1–4.

Exercise 3

You may want to include a summary of skills and qualifications in your resume. These exercises will help you develop your own summary.

Part A

When you have a list or series, it's important to be consistent in word form. This writer has listed several skills, but has used a mix of nouns, verbs, and adjectives. Edit the list to make it consistent. You may combine or delete items.

• have experience managing large staff

• skills in Spanish and English

• effective communicator

• demonstrated leader in school

• experienced in dealing with cultural differences

Part B

Write a skills list for the person described below. Make sure that you are consistent in your list (all nouns or all verbs, for example).

He is a native speaker of Thai. He is also fluent in Japanese and English. He has taken the TOEIC (Test of English in International Communication) and has gotten scores of 855 and 990. He also has computer skills in Microsoft Word, Excel, Frontpage 2000, PowerPoint, and Basic HTML.

Part C

Write your skills and qualifications here. You can list them with bullets or put them in a paragraph.

Exercise 4

The exercises below will help you write your educational experience section.

Part A

This person has a lot of relevant educational experiences and honors, but this section is confusing because the information is not organized or stated well. Combine the education and honors sections. Put everything in reverse chronological order. You may combine items.

Education **B.A. in Communication Engineering**, Osaka University, Suita, Osaka, March 1997

Certificate in English for Business and Internet Technology, University of Washington, Seattle, WA, June 1998

M.A. in Communication Engineering, Osaka University, Suita, Osaka, March 2000

Japanese Language Program, Osaka University for Foreign Students, Minoh, Osaka, March 1994

Honors **Best Score Kusumoto Prize Gold Medal** in Communication Engineering Department, Osaka University, March 1998

Awarded scholarship for academic achievement, 1996–1997

Best Score in Communication Engineering Department, Osaka University, March 2000

Certificate of Achievement in Japanese Language, Osaka University for Foreign students, Minoh, Osaka, March 1994

Part B

What is your education and training? Write it in reverse chronological order. Include degrees, relevant courses, professional training, or honors. Include the dates and the name of the college or program where you studied.

10.2 Action Verbs

When you list your experience in a resume, use action verbs. Action verbs state the actions you took in your job. Here are some examples.

Examples

Management	Development	Information	Communication
administered (something, a program)	created	analyzed (data)	corresponded (*with* someone)
arranged	designed	collected	drafted
approved	developed	evaluated	edited
budgeted for	established	identified	generated
coordinated	founded	interviewed	negotiated (something *with* someone)
directed	introduced	organized	promoted
managed	prepared	researched	publicized
planned		reviewed	represented
set goals		summarized	spoke
supervised			translated
			wrote

Operations	Facilitation	Accomplishments
arranged	adapted	achieved
built	advised	changed
calculated	assisted (someone, *in* something)	decreased
computed	communicated (*with* someone)	expanded
engineered		improved
maintained	facilitated	increased
operated	informed	reduced
programmed	participated in	resolved
repaired	taught	
solved	trained	

Exercise 5

These exercises will help you describe your job experience.

Part A

The lists in this job experience section use a mix of adjective phrases, nouns, and verbs. The verbs are not very specific. Use the action verbs to replace the underlined words below. Write the verbs on the lines.

Section Manager, Marketing Department, Benetton, Taipei, Taiwan

- <u>involved in</u> general management decisions

  a. _____

- <u>discussed plans for</u> integrated marketing strategy

  b. _____

- <u>responsible for</u> database marketing team

  c. _____

- <u>in charge of</u> advertising, events and public relations

  d. _____

- <u>sales went up</u> by 32% in one year

  e. _____

Marketing Executive, Direct Marketing Department, Benetton, Taipei, Taiwan

- <u>responsible for</u> brand management

  f. _____

- <u>chose</u> target consumers

  g. _____

- <u>involved in</u> Direct Marketing project

  h. _____

Marketing Specialist, English Education System Division, Giant Trading Co., Ltd., Taipei, Taiwan

- <u>responsible for</u> marketing strategy and advertising

  i. _____

- <u>did</u> workshop for staff members

  j. _____

Sales Coordinator, Lloyd & Wong, Ltd., Taipei, Taiwan

- <u>did</u> international sales transactions

  k. _____

- <u>did filing</u>

  l. _____

Lesson 10

Part B

What job experience have you had? List it with the most recent first (in reverse chronological order). Include the following information:

- the name of the place where you worked

- what your position was called

- your job duties (think of them as accomplishments) in a bulleted list or paragraph. Use the action verbs on page 75. Quantify your achievements, if possible (e.g., "decreased customer complaints by 15%" or "improved productivity by 10%").

_____

_____

_____

Exercise 6

The activities section is optional. What have you done that might interest an employer? Consider activities such as volunteer work, and special interests.

Write your activities here. Remember to list them in a consistent way (all verbs, all adjectives, or all nouns).

_____

_____

_____

Exercise 7

Use the information you worked on above to write your resume. Your word processing program may have a template for resumes. In some Microsoft Word programs, a resume template is under File, New, Other Documents.

Lesson 11. Cover Letters for Resumes

Exercise 1

"Cover letters" are letters that people send to companies with their resumes. Read the two cover letters below, and then answer the following question.

If you were Mr. Lee, which person would you contact? Why?

A

Tomoko Martin
8105 50th Street N.W.
Davis, CA 95616

August 18, 200X

Sung Woo Lee
Human Resources Director
Port of Seattle
Pier 55
Seattle, WA 98190

Dear Mr. Lee:

I understand that the Port of Seattle is expanding to accommodate the increase in ships that will be using Seattle as their base of operations. My fluency in three languages, experience working with international visitors, and office skills would allow me to assist your department in this new arena.

As the enclosed resume shows, I have the skills and experience to work in any administrative position. I would also welcome the opportunity to use my interpersonal skills in representing the Port of Seattle to visitors.

I will contact your office early next week to see if it would be convenient for you to meet with me to discuss my qualifications in person.

Yours truly,
Tomoko Martin
Tomoko Martin

B

280 Winslow Way
Bainbridge, WA 98110

August 10, 200X

Port of Seattle
Pier 55
Seattle, WA 98190

To Whom It May Concern:

Enclosed is my resume. I am interested in applying for any administrative jobs available in your organization.

As my resume shows, I have a B.A. in English from Yale University. I am looking for a job that will be challenging and that will give me lots of opportunities to move ahead in my career.

I look forward to hearing from you regarding an interview for any openings you have in your company.

Sincerely,
Mary Hogan
Mary Hogan

11.1 Cover Letters

The cover letter is also a marketing tool. Like the resume, it "sells" you. It explains to the potential employer how you will help the company. It does not restate the information in your resume. Instead, it highlights your skills and assets. Also, it shows your interest in the company. A good cover letter must look professional. And it must be specific, relating your information directly to the job you want in the company you are applying to.

There are three types of cover letters:

1. A referral (when someone has suggested that you contact a specific person about job possibilities)

2. A response to an ad (when you are answering a job posting or announcement)

3. An unsolicited letter (when you don't know anyone at the company and have no idea what kinds of jobs are available)

Guidelines

Format

1. Keep your cover letter to one page.

2. Use a standard business letter format, such as block left or modified block.

3. Try to find out the name of the person who will read the letter. Telephone the company to ask or get a referral. To get a referral, ask an employee you know. If you do not know a specific person's name, use a title, such as Human Resources Manager or Personnel Director, instead of the impersonal To Whom It May Concern.

4. If possible, put your cover letter and resume on the same kind of paper and use a similar font size and style. Sign your letter in black or blue pen.

Content

1. Use a positive and professional tone. This is the first sample of your writing skills that the employer will see, so make it as perfect as your resume.

2. Begin with the reason you are writing. Mention how you learned about the position. If someone referred you, state that first. If this is an unsolicited letter, use a strong beginning to attract the readers' attention.

3. In the main paragraph(s) of the letter, show how hiring you will benefit the company. Be specific. Show how you and your qualifications differ from other job applicants.

4. In the last paragraph, request an interview. Also, suggest a time when you are available or when you will telephone to arrange an interview.

Lesson 11

Exercise 2

The cover letter below is divided into seven parts. Each part has three statement choices. Circle the letter of the best statement for each part.

---

430 Memorial Drive
Houston, TX 77027

October 4, 200X

Mr. Andrew Clark
Human Resources Director
DRM Laboratories
2000 Technology Drive
Stanton, TX 79782

Dear Andrew:
1. (a) Dear Human Resources Director;
   (b) Dear Mr. Clark:
   (c)

Have you found someone yet to work as a database designer?
2. (a) I am writing in response to the job announcement in the paper for a database designer.
   (b) I am pleased to be able to answer your advertisement for a database designer.
   (c)

As you can see from the enclosed resume, I designed the database for our office.
3. (a) When you look at my resume, you will see that I have the right qualifications for the job.
   (b) My two years of work as a database programmer and my previous years of data entry
   (c) experience have given me first-hand knowledge of the skills and challenges that an organization faces when trying to design a new database.

I also have an associate degree in information technology.
4. (a) I had an outstanding grade point average in my coursework for my degree.
   (b) In addition to my practical experience, my academic work has given me the theoretical
   (c) background to be able to apply my experience effectively.

In addition to these qualifications, my recommendations will attest to my strong
5. (a) interpersonal skills.
       I have always wanted to work at your company.
   (b) My experience, education, and ability to work effectively with others will help me contribute
   (c) to your organization.

I would appreciate having the opportunity to meet with you to find out the specific needs at
6. (a) DRM Laboratories.
       I would be very happy to talk with you about my background.
   (b) It would be my great pleasure to have the opportunity to have an interview for this position.
   (c)

I will telephone your office on Monday about the possibility of an interview.
7. (a) I hope to hear from you soon about an interview.
   (b) Please call me to let me know when I can come in for an interview.
   (c)

Sincerely yours,

Mark Kaminsky

Mark Kaminsky

Enclosure

Exercise 3

Follow these steps to develop your own cover letter. Remember that you must prepare before you write.

1. Find out the name and position of the person you should apply to.

2. Research the company. Is it growing? Does it want people with certain skills? Get information that might help you get a job there.

3. Think about your qualifications. What skills and experience do you have that could help the company. List them here.

   _____

   _____

4. Start your cover letter. Write the addresses and date. Be sure to use correct position titles and a correct greeting.

5. Now, begin the text, or body of the letter. Start by saying how you found out about the job (an advertisement or referral). If a job was not advertised, and no one referred you, start by saying something to get the reader's attention. Say something that will interest him or her in your application.

6. Use your notes from question 2 to write the next paragraph(s) of your letter.

7. In your last paragraph, say how you will follow up. Remember that it is your job to take the next step and contact the company.

8. Edit your letter carefully to make sure that you have used correct grammar and punctuation.

Lesson 12. Follow-Up Letters

Exercise 1

Answer the questions about these follow-up letters.

1. Put a check if the letter includes information or sentences about the following.

	Letter A	Letter B
a. thanks	____	____
b. what the writer enjoyed or found interesting	____	____
c. a summary of the writer's qualifications	____	____
d. an expression of interest in working for the company	____	____

2. Which letter would impress you more if you were the person deciding about a job candidate?

A

Rick Stevens
Box 456
3400 Walnut Street
Philadelphia, PA 19107

May 5, 200X

Mr. Andrew Clark
Human Resources Director
DRM Laboratories
2000 Technology Drive
Stanton, TX 79782

Dear Mr. Clark:

Thank you for taking the time to talk with me yesterday and for showing me around your headquarters. I appreciated having the opportunity to see your facilities and meet some of your employees.

I was very impressed with your company's commitment to producing high-quality products and to creating a positive work environment for employees. The more I see and learn about DRM, the more I hope to be able to work there.

I look forward to hearing from you.

Sincerely,
Rick Stevens
Richard Stevens

B

17 Manchester Road
Brookline, MA 02146
May 8, 200X

Karl Mueller
Pacific Cruises
519 S. Figueroa
Los Angeles, CA 90071

Dear Mr. Mueller:

I appreciated having the opportunity to meet with you today to tell you more about my experience and qualifications. After talking with you, I feel very strongly that your company would be a good match for me. I think that my experience in customer service and my interest in pursuing a career in the travel industry would enable me to do an excellent job in your organization.

I hope to hear from you soon.

Thank you.

Yours truly,
Jerene Tan
Jerene Tan

12.1 Follow-up Letters

Interviews are a common part of the job application process. In some countries, it is also common to do "information interviews" when you are deciding on a career. In both cases, write a follow-up letter to the person you met with.

Guidelines

> Write the letter as soon as possible (within a couple of days following the interview).

> The most important part of the letter is your expression of thanks and appreciation. Review the expressions in table 3.1 on page 16. The letter does not have to be long.

> In a letter following a job interview, you do not need to restate your qualifications for the job. The interviewer evaluated your qualifications at the time of the interview, so this is not necessary.

Exercise 2

Write a follow up letter. If you don't have a real visit or interview to write about, imagine a situation in which you might need to write this kind of a letter.

Appendices

> > > > > > > > > > > > > >

Appendix 1 Sample Letters

Block-Left Style

Firstname Lastname
100 A Street, Apt. 100
City, State Zip

August 5, 200X

Mr./Ms. First name Lastname
Title or Department
Company Name
2000 Street, Suite 100
City, State Zip

Dear Mr./Ms. Lastname:

I am writing to find out information about accommodations and meeting rooms at your hotel. I'm making arrangements for a conference that would involve about 200 people, so I'd appreciate information about group rates, meeting rooms, and catering. Also, please let me know about availability during the month of April. The conference would start on a Tuesday and end on Friday morning.

We would like to offer our conference attendees some options for afternoon and day trips in the area. Does your hotel make these arrangements or is there another company I should contact?

I would appreciate any information you could give me.

Sincerely,

Firstname Lastname

Firstname Lastname
Position

Modified Block-Left Style

Firstname Lastname
100 A Street, Apt. 100
City, State Zip

August 5, 200X

Mr./Ms. Firstname Lastname
Title or Department
Company Name
2000 Street, Suite 100
City, State Zip

Dear Mr./Ms. Lastname:

I am writing to find out information about accommodations and meeting rooms at your hotel. I'm making arrangements for a conference that would involve about 200 people, so I'd appreciate information about group rates, meeting rooms, and catering. Also, please let me know about availability during the month of April. The conference would start on a Tuesday and end on Friday morning.

We would like to offer our conference attendees some options for afternoon and day trips in the area. Does your hotel make these arrangements or is there another company I should contact?

I would appreciate any information you could give me.

Sincerely,

Firstname Lastname

Firstname Lastname
Position

Simplified Letter Style

Simplified letter format is often used for mass mailing (the same letter sent to many people, usually to inform them of a new product or some important information).

- Instead of a greeting, use a heading.
- Leave two spaces above and below this heading to set it apart.
- Instead of a closing, write your signature.
- Put your name and title on the same line and in capital letters below your signature.

Company Letterhead
with address / telephone / fax

August 5, 200X

Mr./Ms. Firstname Lastname
Title or Department
Company Name
2000 Street
City, State Zip

THE PERFECT RESORT

Are you looking for the perfect vacation resort? Are you looking for a good investment and possible retirement home?

Sea Island offers the perfect spot for exciting vacations and for luxurious retirement. Located just 35 minutes from the Tampa airport, Sea Island combines the relaxation of a resort with all the conveniences of the city. Living options include condominiums, townhouses, and villas—all with pools, hot tubs, and athletic facilities nearby. Visit the spa, go deep-sea fishing, or play a round of golf—your possibilities are endless!

Call now for more information about our special promotional rate. You won't regret it!

Firstname Lastname

FIRSTNAME LASTNAME, TITLE

Appendix 1

Personal Letter

A personal letter can be on letterhead stationery and can be handwritten or typed. A return address may be included at the top of the page.

August 5, 200X

Dear Firstname,

Thank you for your card. I was quite surprised to get this promotion, but I'm looking forward to starting my new position. I'm glad that we'll be able to continue working together.

Soo you on tho 15th!

Best regards,

Firstname

E-Mail

Date: Mon, 23 Apr 200X 10:55:24 -0700 (PDT)
From: Jose Antonio Martinez <joseam@videtron.ca>
To: info@mh.com
CC:
Subject: Business Books

I own a book distribution company in Colombia, and I'm interested in adding some new titles to our English language selections. I understand that your company has a wide variety of business titles. Could you suggest a few titles that have been successful in other international settings? I'm particularly interested in the types of books that people can read on their own to develop new skills.

Also, please let me know about prices, terms of payment, and shipping costs.

Thank you for your assistance.

Jose Antonio Martinez
Carrera 8 No. 26b-14
Bogota 2, Colombia, S.A.

Appendix 2 Punctuation Styles

In "mixed" punctuation, use a colon after the greeting and a comma after the closing. In a personal letter (to a friend) or in an e-mail message, you can use a comma instead of a colon after the greeting. Mixed punctuation is used in business letters in the United States.

Mixed Punctuation

Dear Ms. Smith:

xxxxxxxxxxxx xx xxxxxx x
xxxxxxxxxxxxxxxxxx. xxx xx x
xxxxxx.

Sincerely yours,
Caroline Martin
Caroline Martin

In "open punctuation," do not punctuate the greeting or closing. This style is not used in the United States.

Open Punctuation

Dear Ms. Smith

xxxxxxxxxxxx xx xxxxxx x
xxxxxxxxxxxxxxxxxx. xxx xx x
xxxxxx.

Sincerely yours
Caroline Martin
Caroline Martin

When you don't know the person you are writing to, use the "simplified" letter style. Use a heading, not a greeting. Do not use a closing. This style is used for mass mailings, such as announcements for new company products or services.

Simplified Letter

INFORMATION REQUEST

xxxxxxxxxxxx xx xxxxxx x
xxxxxxxxxxxxxxxxxx. xxx xx x
xxxxxx.

Caroline Martin
CAROLINE MARTIN

Appendix 3 Abbreviations for the United States and Canada

United States

Alabama	AL	Kentucky	KY	Ohio	OH
Alaska	AK	Louisiana	LA	Oklahoma	OK
Arizona	AZ	Maine	ME	Oregon	OR
Arkansas	AR	Maryland	MD	Pennsylvania	PA
California	CA	Massachusetts	MA	Puerto Rico	PR
Colorado	CO	Michigan	MI	Rhode Island	RI
Connecticut	CT	Minnesota	MN	South Carolina	SC
Delaware	DE	Mississippi	MS	South Dakota	SD
District of Columbia	DC	Missouri	MO	Tennessee	TN
Florida	FL	Montana	MT	Texas	TX
Georgia	GA	Nebraska	NE	Utah	UT
Guam	GU	Nevada	NV	Vermont	VT
Hawaii	HI	New Hampshire	NH	Virgin Islands	VI
Idaho	ID	New Jersey	NJ	Virginia	VA
Illinois	IL	New Mexico	NM	Washington	WA
Indiana	IN	New York	NY	West Virginia	WV
Iowa	IA	North Carolina	NC	Wisconsin	WI
Kansas	KA	North Dakota	ND	Wyoming	WY

Canada

Alberta	AB	Newfoundland	NF	Quebec	QC
British Columbia	BC	Northwest Territories	NT	Saskatchewan	SK
Labrador	LB	Nova Scotia	NS	Yukon Territory	YT
Manitoba	MB	Ontario	ON		
New Brunswick	NB	Prince Edward Island	PE		

Appendix 4 Capitalization Rules

Guidelines	Examples
Use capital letters for the following: **1.** names and titles Note: When the title is general, do not use a capital letter.	Bill Casey Ms. Caroline E. Thompson David Bell Personnel Director He is the personnel director of the Boeing company.
2. names of places, languages, and people from a country or area Note: Use all capital letters for the abbreviations of states and provinces. Note: Capitalize direction words (north, south, east, west) when they are specific.	We have sales representatives in South America. The directions are in English and Spanish. They visited five African countries. They tested the motor on Clear Lake in the Rocky Mountains. San Francisco, CA Vancouver, BC Our East Coast sales representative is Ann Clark. The company moved west in 2003.
3. names of streets, buildings, companies, and other organizations Note: Prepositions and articles are not capitalized.	Cartons, Inc. Energy Center, Suite 200 2100 S. Poydras Street National Association of Sales Representatives Society for a Free Marketplace
4. names of days, months, and holidays	I'll be in Seattle from Wednesday, December 1, through Christmas.
5. names of products	Pepsi and Coca-Cola are both colas. I am experienced in all Microsoft Office applications.

Guidelines	Examples
6. titles of books, movies, courses, and degrees Note: When the course or degree is general, it is not capitalized.	They produced *Lord of the Rings*. Management 301 will be taught by James Fox, Ph.D. I received an M.B.A. I have a master's degree in business administration. He taught information management in the business school.
7. names of religions	It is a Moslem tradition, but it is also a custom in Christianity.
8. nouns followed by numbers and letters that make a title	Invoice No. 4437 I have enclosed Form B as requested.
9. words in quotation marks showing that they are named.	We shipped the product in an envelope stamped "Photographs Enclosed." Even though the package was marked "Fragile," the glass inside was broken.
10. the first word of a sentence	Thank you for your help.
11. the word "I"	On July 15, I will be in New York.

Appendix 5 Common First Names

First Names, Female		First Names, Male	
Abigail	Kaitlyn	Alex (male or female)	Lee (male or female, either first or last)
Alex (male or female)	Karen	Antonio	Mark
Alison	Katerina	Andrew	Martin (either)
Anna, Anne, Ann	Katherine	Bill	Marty (male or female)
Arlene	Kay	Bob	Matthew
Ashley	Kayla	Brandon	Max
Brenda	Kim (either first or last)	Carl	Michael
Carol	Kris (male or female)	Carlos	Miguel
Carolina	Laura/Lauren	Chris (male or female)	Nicholas
Caroline	Lee (male or female, either first or last)	Christopher	Paul
Chris (male or female)	Madison	Daniel	Peter
Christina	Marcia	Dave/David	Robert
Christine	Maria	Dennis	Ron
Diana	Martha	Edward	Ryan (either first or last)
Elizabeth	Marty (male or female)	Francis (male or female)	Sam
Emily	Mary	Fred	Sergio
Emma	Megan	George	Shen
Frances	Melanie	Jacob	Stephen/Steven
Francis (male or female)	Nicole	James	Thomas
Fredericka	Olivia	Jim	Tom
Gill	Patricia	John	Tyler
Grace	Rachel	Jose	William
Greta	Sarah	Joseph	Zachary
Hannah	Stacy	Joshua	
Hillary	Susan	Justin	
Jennifer	Takako	Kris (male or female)	
Jessica	Tracy		
Jill	Victoria		
Judy			
Julia			
Julie			

Glossary

a.s.a.p./ ASAP—as soon as possible

abbreviation—short form, initials

administrative assistant—secretary

application—form or set of materials turned in to apply for something; software for a specific use

area—region, department or functional group

attachment—a document that is sent with an e-mail message

batch—group of items being worked on at one time

benefit—do well from something, get something positive

benefits—what an employee gets from a company in addition to money, e.g., insurance, retirement pay

brochure—promotional information

budget (n. and v.)—plan regarding finances

client—person who uses the services of a company

closing—the phrase that goes before a signature in a letter

colleague—co-worker

compensation—money or some special arrangement to make up for expenses or problems that someone had

conference call—telephone call with more than two people participating (also known as a "telecon")

co-worker—someone who works with you

customer—person who buys something from you (usually in a store)

deadline—date when something needs to be finished

department—section of an organization

discuss—talk about (note: discuss something; talk *about* something)

distributor (n.)—middle person; the person or organization that moves a product into the market

enclosure—something that is sent with a letter or in an envelope

expand—grow

facility (-ies)—building(s) where something is produced or where a company operates

full time—working a full job

greeting—the salutation in a letter or e-mail

guidelines—a description of how things should work

heading—the name of a subject or topic

inquiry/inquiries—question(s)

invoice—statement of money owed or paid

maintain—keep up, keep in good condition

manager—the person in charge

order—(v.) demand or request to buy something; (n.) what has been bought

option—possible choice

policy—a rule or decision about procedure

position—a job category

potential (adj.)—possible; (n.) possibility

product—something that is made or manufactured

product line—a group of things offered for sale

promote (v.), promotion (n.)—work to advertise a product or draw people's attention to it; move an employee up to a better job

purchase—(n.) something you buy, (v.) buy

purchasing—in charge of buying

receive—get

recommendation—letter or conversation in which one person says whether someone else is a good candidate for an opening in a school or business

sales representative—a person in charge of selling for a company

solution—way to solve a problem

specific—not general

stack—items arranged one on top of another

staff—(noncount) a group of people (staff members) who work for an organization, a department, or a person

status—current position; position in relation to other people

talk about—discuss

team—group of people working together

telecon—telephone conference (meeting)

term—length of time; specific details of an agreement

warranty—guarantee

workmanship—the way something is built

Index